Walking Strathspey, Moray, Banff and Buchan

Clan Walk Guides

Walking
Strathspey
Moray, Banff
and Buchan

Walking Scotland Series
Volume 16

Mary Welsh
and
Christine Isherwood

First published by Clan Books, 2009

ISBN 978 1873597 32 3
Text and Illustrations
© Mary Welsh
and
Christine Isherwood 2009

The authors wish to express their gratitude to Jennifer Outhwaite
for her help in preparing this volume

Clan Books
Clandon House
The Cross, Doune
Perthshire
FK16 6BE

Printed and bound in Great Britain by
Bell & Bain Ltd., Glasgow

Publishers Note

Our authors have produced a substantial new piece to fit into the jig-saw of *Walking Scotland Series* guides, with a well-balanced range of walks from the headwaters of the Spey to the Buchan coast.

Much of the terrain comprises highland estates whose moors and mountains are legally accessible to walkers under the Land Reform Act, 2003. Landowners, however, continue to exercise their right to shoot game birds and stalk deer over these hills, and it is essential, during the sporting season, from August 12th to October 20th to pay attention to notices on estate tracks and to respect warnings from responsible estate personnel. Many properties have a telephone helpline to check whether it is safe to walk the hill on a particular day. Sundays are safe almost everywhere. If in doubt, ask someone who lives locally, and if you have a dog, keep it on a lead.

The Authors' Golden Rules
for Good, Safe Walking

- Wear suitable clothes and take adequate waterproofs.
- Walk in strong footwear; walking boots are advisable.
- Carry the relevant map and a compass and know how to use them.
- Carry a whistle; remember six long blasts repeated at one minute intervals is the distress signal.
- Do not walk alone, and tell someone where you are going.
- If mist descends, return.
- Keep all dogs under strict control. Observe all "No Dogs" notices – they are there for very good reasons.

In all volumes of the WALKING SCOTLAND series, the authors make every effort to ensure accuracy, but changes can occur after publication. Reports of such changes are welcomed by the publisher. Neither the publisher nor the authors can accept responsibility for errors, omissions or any loss or injury.

Contents

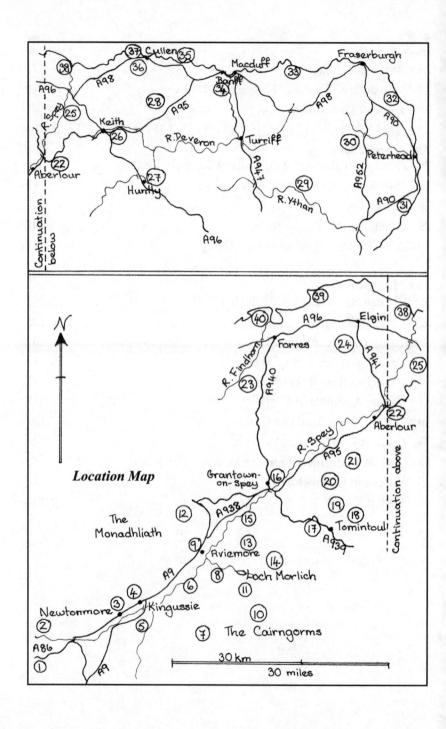

Location Map

1

Falls of Pattack and Kinlochlaggan

Park in layby 110yds/100m east of the bridge to Gallovie farm, grid ref 556899. Access this by the A86 from Newtonmore to Spean Bridge, about 6 miles/9.5km west of Laggan.

There are two Falls of Pattack, an Upper and a Lower Fall. This walk visits the **Upper Fall**, but a short walk from a Forestry car park east of the start of the walk takes you to the Lower Fall. The Pattack, the river of potholes, rises on Ben Alder and descends tumultuously.

Ardverikie Estate featured in the TV series 'Monarch of the Glen'. The big house was Glenbogle House. The estate is very welcoming to walkers, and although deer stalking does take place you are unlikely to be in the way on this walk.

1 Walk west along the road, with care, and cross to take the track, signed to Gallovie Farm, on the south side of the road. Go over the bridge and wind round to the right through splendid estate woodlands, ignoring a track on the right signed to 'sawmill'. Follow the blue waymark, which directs you ahead and uphill to the farm. Go between the buildings, then left and over the crest of the hill into the forest. Continue ahead on the obvious track, following

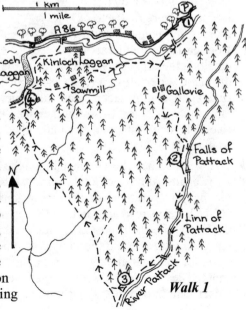

Walk 1

another waymark, until you reach a sign on the left for the Falls of Pattack. Follow the small path down to the river and along the bank until there is a good view back to the splendid falls. You will want to pause here and enjoy the spectacular fall before you return to the forest track and turn left.

Upper Falls of Pattack

2 Go over a ladder stile beside a deer gate. The forest is now to your right and the ground to the left is open. The path comes near to the river, which is very attractive with many small rapids, and where you might spot dippers. Ignore a narrow bridge and go on along the good sandy track. Beyond a deer grid the track crosses the river on a sturdy wooden bridge and carries on along the far side. Soon you reach the Linn of Pattack, a small but dramatic waterfall in a rocky cleft. Further on the track crosses the river again and the steep sided valley opens out, with views of mountains in the distance. Cross another deer grid and wind round above the river. The double-topped mountain ahead is Geal Charn, one of many so named.

3 The forest comes close to the path on the right and then turns abruptly away again. At this point take a track which goes off on the right, following the forest fence and climbing gently across the moorland, with Geal Charn away to your left. At the top of the moor there is a gate into the forest with a stile beside it, which you take. Carry on down with the fence on your left and the lodgepole pine of the forest on your right. Look for roe deer among the trees and, outside the forest, you might spot red deer feeding in the hollows. Eventually the track goes through a deer gate into conifers and is soon joined by another from the left.

Head on down, following the main track until it joins a metalled road where Loch Laggan appears through the trees. Turn right.

4 Stroll on along the road, the approach drive to Ardverikie House, as it comes nearer to the loch and runs along above the shore. There are splendid views across the water to Creag Meagaidh, with the distinctive shape of the Window now very obvious. Go round a rocky bluff and take a forest track on the right, leading away from the water. If you have time to spare, you might like to go on along the road to come to a fine sandy beach, which stretches along the head of the loch and is a lovely place for a picnic. To continue the walk return through the fine mature estate woodlands, with noble and Douglas firs, Norway spruce and Scots pine. Go through the sawmill and on to a gate out of the woodland. The track winds across damp fields, with the River Pattack, very calm and gentle here, on your left. You may meet Highland garrons, shaggy ponies used in stalking; they are usually very friendly. Go through the gate passed on your outward route, turn left and retrace your steps to your car.

Red Deer

Practicals

Type of walk: Good paths and tracks all the way. The River Pattack is spectacular.

Complete distance:	6 miles/9.5km
Time:	3–4 hours
Maps:	OS Explorer 393/Landranger 42

2

Geal Charn

There is room for two cars parked carefully on the verge where the road turns sharp left to cross the Spey just below Spey Dam, grid ref 584937. Alternatively there is parking further up the road. To reach this take the minor road which leaves the A86 at Laggan and runs west to Spey Dam and Garva Bridge.

Geal Charn, 3,055ft/926m, is one of the Munros of the **Monadhliath (Grey Mountains),** the wide area of high ground west of Upper Strathspey. Much of this area is difficult of access; although there are rights of way across it, it can be very bleak and remote. The reward for venturing up here is the wide spacious view over so much wild land. There are four Munros in the Monadhliath, all of them along the south-east edge behind Laggan and Glen Banchor.

Geal Charn means White Hill or White Cairn. It is an extremely common mountain name in this part of the Highlands; there are four Munros called Geal Charn, all in the Cairngorm and Laggan area, and 19 Geal Charns altogether.

Lochan a' Choire

1 Go through the gate by the parking area and walk on along a track beside the river towards the dam. Wind round right, pass through another gate and climb the river terrace, with ruins below to the left. Harebells and devil's-bit scabious grow on the banks in summer. Go through a deer gate beside a plantation and carry on up the track into the wide valley of the Markie Burn. Beinn Sgiath looms on the left with Geal Charn tucked in behind it. Go uphill steadily for about two miles, through two more deer gates, and down to the bank of the Markie Burn opposite the entry of a major tributary, the Piper's Burn. If the river is low, cross here on stones just above the confluence. However if the river is high this may not be possible, in which case continue on the path, a right of way, along the riverbank to a bridge about ½ mile/1 km upstream and then make your way back along the far side, slanting uphill.

Walk 2

2 From the first crossing point, take a path which goes up beside the Piper's Burn, past a fine waterfall. Go through a gate in the fence and follow the path up through the corrie, keeping to the bank of the right branch of the burn. As you get higher the path becomes less distinct, but make for the ridge to your right by the easiest route. Scan the skyline from time to time for golden eagles.

3 On reaching the ridge, which is broad and has some peat hags to avoid, turn left and work your way in and out between rocky knolls up to the summit plateau. This gives very pleasant walking over short grass and

stones for about ½ mile/1km to the fine cairn. The view from here is splendid and extensive.

Golden Eagle

4 Leave the summit in a south-easterly direction, heading towards Beinn Sgiath and keeping well to the right of the cliffs which edge the plateau. Go down the slope, choosing the easiest gradient, into the steep-sided notch (or window) between Geal Charn and Beinn Sgiath. Walk left round the edge of a small pool and over the lip, slanting carefully down the steep slope. Soon the gradient eases. Take bits of paths down through grass, flowers and rocks towards Lochan a'Choire cradled below. There are cliffs on both sides but the way down, though rough in places, is delightful. Follow the path, of sorts, round the shore of the lochan to the outflow, Piper's Burn, and then continue beside it across the corrie floor. Soon all sight of the lochan disappears; it is really well hidden in its corner of the corrie. Cross the Piper's Burn at a convenient place and walk on downhill to its tributary burn which you cross to rejoin your outward path. Go on down over the Markie Burn and retrace your steps to your car.

Practicals

Type of walk: The way through the corrie is boggy in wet weather and there is a short area of peat hags on the ridge, but much of the walk is on good tracks or well-drained grass. After heavy or prolonged rain you will not be able to ford the Markie Burn so use the bridge upstream. As for all Munros, take care. The country to the north is wild and trackless.

Complete distance: 10 miles/16km
Time: 6–7 hours
Maps: OS Explorer 401/Landranger 35

NB The Glen Markie track is a right of way, but before climbing Geal Charn during the stalking season (12th August to 20th October) check with the estate if it is safe to do so on 01528 544222.

The Wildcat Trail, Newtonmore

Park in a layby by the Bridge of Aultlarie, ¼ mile/0.5km beyond the Highland Folk Museum, grid ref 729999. Access this using the A86 through the centre of Newtonmore and out to the north towards Kingussie.

Newtonmore is a direct translation of the Gaelic Baile Ur an t-Sleibh, which means the new township on the moor. It was developed in the early 19th century. The area had always been well populated, with many small crofting townships; the walk passes the remains of some of them. In 1765 the Duke of Gordon had a bridge built over the Spey. Gradually people began to move in from the outlying areas to build new homes around the road leading to the bridge and develop trades other than crofting. The railway was built in 1863 and this brought more people, more trade and eventually tourists, to contribute to a thriving village.

The Wildcat Trail was developed by the Newtonmore Community Woodland Trust. Leaflets describing walks in the vicinity are available from their shop on Newtonmore main street. The wildcat is used by Newtonmore on its village symbol. These wildcat

Waterfall on Allt Laraidh   C.K.Isherwood

signs welcome visitors to the village, which has
hosted Wildcat Festivals in recent
years. The area has links
with Clan Chattan, a
group that includes
the Macphersons, who
have their museum in
Newtonmore, and these
clans use the wildcat in
their crest.

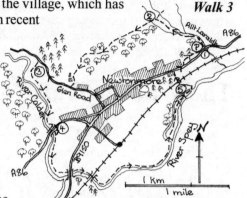

1 From the layby, take a
grassy track which curves
into woods by the river, the
Allt Laraidh. Go through a small gate and continue along the riverbank
through a narrow wooded valley. Soon a fine waterfall comes into
view. Pass through a gate, cross a bridge over a tributary burn, then
climb the bank beside the waterfall. Admire the view behind you to
the Cairngorms, then go on through another gate. To your left there
is a signpost, which is not on the clear grassy path you are following,
but walk across towards it and you will find the remains of an old
township, with a plaque on a boulder describing the history of the area.
Return to the track and at a T-junction turn left.

2 Cross a burn on a footbridge and climb the far bank to a
small gate into a recent plantation. Keep along the north
edge of the trees, crossing several rides each of which
has two kissing gates. Make a diversion left when you
reach a seat to visit the remains of a hut circle. Then go
on into old twisted birch trees. Look out across the moor
to see several finely-built cairns, and behind them the
high mountains of the Monadhliath. Eventually the path
develops into a track, winding round the edge of the
wood and then bearing left to become an access track
for three cottages. Carry on down the track to a minor road
(the Glen Road) and turn right, up into Glen Banchor, through
scattered mature birch. Where the road begins to dip, look for
a signpost on the left, and descend the beautiful grassy path
towards the River Calder. There are two plaques on boulders
detailing the history of the area; this was a settlement called
Milton and you can see the remains of a mill as well as the
lade, and other house remains scattered on the hillside. The
view up Glen Banchor is superb.

Melancholy Thistle

3 Descend to the side of the River Calder and bear left through a gate into woodland. Open areas have been replanted with native trees by the Newtonmore Community Woodland Trust. Continue along the path, which stays fairly level, shelf-like, as the river enters a gorge and descends in splendid rapids. On the far side stands Creag Dubh, a dramatic hill, with woods clothing its lower slopes. The path winds round left as the gorge opens out. Ignore the next gate and instead turn sharp right down steps to regain the river-bank. Pass through a gate and continue beside the river, with alders to your right. Look for common sandpipers and grey wagtails.

4 At Calder Bridge, the main road goes over the river. Cross the road and walk ahead through a metalled entry to a field, then immediately turn right through a small gate onto the river-bank. Carry on along the path on the top of the embankment to the confluence of the Calder and the Spey. This is not easy to see because of a proliferation of sand and gravel banks, many of which are covered in alders. Turn the corner and follow the stiled way under the B-road bridge and then the railway bridge. The land is a floodplain, with sand and gravel showing through the vegetation and signs of water-borne debris in the trees. Cross stepping stones onto an island, Eilean na Cluanaich, and carry on through the alders with an ox-bow lake to your left. Cross more stepping stones, followed by a bridge.

5 Turn left to walk beside the burn, on your left, to cross a bridge over the railway. Head on along the now metalled road out to join the main road. Cross and walk right along the pavement, with the Highland Folk Museum across the road. After the last house climb steps and follow an attractive path through pines and birches which brings you back to the layby where you left your car.

Common Sandpiper

Practicals

Type of walk: Good paths or tracks through splendid woodland and beside fine rivers. Bicycles are not allowed and dogs must be kept on a lead.

Complete distance:	7 miles/11.5km
Time:	3–4 hours
Maps:	OS Explorer 402/Landranger 35

4

Loch Gynack and Creag Bheag, Kingussie

Park in Ardvonie free car park, grid ref 755007, signed off A86 which runs through the centre of Kingussie.

The name **Kingussie** is derived from the Gaelic, and means 'The head of the pine wood', indicating its position near the edge of the Caledonian pine forest in Strathspey. It is the ancient capital of Badenoch and is built on the site of an old settlement dating from 565 AD, when a chapel dedicated to St Columba was founded here. In the late 18th Century the Duke of Gordon advertised for tradesmen and craftsmen to settle in the town and it became the centre of a spinning and weaving industry for a time.

Mountain Hares are smaller than the brown hare and are more likely to be seen feeding in groups. In winter they moult into a completely white coat, which is a very good camouflage if there is snow, but otherwise makes them rather conspicuous against the dark heather. They feed mainly on heather and mountain grasses, and are preyed on by foxes, eagles and wildcats.

Mountain Hares

1 Return from the car park to Gynack Road and turn left. Just beyond the next bend take a signed path, on the right, and go down steps to cross the Gynack Burn on a wooden footbridge. Go up steps on the far side

and turn left to walk through woodland of hazel and birch, carpeted with woodrush. Here you might spot red squirrels. Emerge from the trees and bear right to join the road and turn left along it. Do not take the signed path on the left at a stone cairn, but carry on along the road, with the turbulent river foaming

Walk 4

over little falls on your left. Go through a gateway and walk on with a pinewood now on the right, then the golf course.

2 Take the path on the left at a signpost directing you across part of the golf course (where you are advised not to linger) and cross a bridge over the burn. Turn right along the bank and climb steeply up beside a fence to approach the golf course again. Follow signs directing you right, out of harm's way, along the far side of a small hill. Climb to a col and then walk along the crest of the low ridge through fine deciduous trees. At the end of the ridge go between two derelict buildings into a pinewood. Suddenly, as the trees thin out, you have your first glimpse of hidden Loch Gynack. The path descends to a gate and out onto the open hill. Enjoy the views along the loch, with Creag Bheag to your left and Creag Mhor across the water to your right. Look for goldeneye and mallards.

3 The waymarked path now goes uphill to the left, but this walk continues along a clear unmarked path that runs above the loch shore, through the heather and into boggy birch woodland. Towards the end of the loch the path comes out onto the open hillside again and begins a steady gentle ascent to the top of a spur. Slightly below you here, on a green, grassy area, are the remains of an old township that you may wish to explore. Then take an indistinct path, acutely left, going up the hill into the heather. Follow this path as far as you can and where it becomes vague, make for a rocky knoll, then climb a steep terrace beyond it. Follow an animal path that runs, left, along the edge of the terrace until you meet a distinct path, which suddenly appears through the heather, leading you to the final steep ascent.

17

4 As you climb look out for red grouse and mountain hares. At the top, the path winds across the rocky ridge, in and out of hollows and over knolls. The first spectacular rocky top is the same height as the official summit but it is worth carrying on to the proper summit cairn, joining a wider path on the way. The views over Speyside and the Monadhliath are splendid.

Loch Gynack

5 When you are ready to descend, take the wide waymarked path back the way you came. Keep to it as it begins to go downhill, winding round the many crags on this side of the hill, bringing you to the top of a pine plantation where there is a signpost. Go through a gate and on ahead. It is hard to distinguish between the path and a burn at first, but soon the burn plunges off to the right and the path continues round the hillside as a lovely needle-carpeted terrace, gradually descending. At the foot of the hill, bear right, down to a gate. Beyond, turn right down a track behind houses to join a road and carry on down. Where West Terrace goes off right, turn left and slant down a long slope, or down steps, to cross a recreation area back to Ardvonie car park.

Practicals

Type of walk: Mostly on good paths. The section by the loch can be boggy and from there up the hill is relatively trackless with steep bits

Complete distance:	5 miles/8km
Time:	2–3 hours
Maps:	OS Explorer 402/Landranger 35

Insh Marshes and Glen Tromie

Park in the RSPB and Badenoch Way car park at Insh Marshes Nature Reserve, grid ref 774998. To access this take the B970 from Kingussie, signed to Ruthven Barracks. The car park is beyond the barracks.

The **RSPB's Insh Marshes Reserve** is a wetland of international importance. The Spey floods it repeatedly in winter, when hundreds of whooper swans and greylag geese from Iceland visit and hen harriers use the area for roosting. In summer it is a network of pools and ditches where lapwings, redshank, snipe and curlews breed. There is also a large breeding population of goldeneye. Roe deer, red squirrels and otters can also be seen.

Ruthven Barracks is well worth a visit before or after this walk. It was built in 1719 following the Jacobite Rebellion of 1715, to house the government infantry. The barracks consists of two large houses where the soldiers were quartered, and a stable block. It changed hands several times before being burnt down in 1746, after Culloden. The mound where it stands was previously used for a succession of castles.

Ruthven Barracks

1 Climb the steps out of the car park, heading for Invertromie. Turn left at the top to visit the information viewpoint, a spacious hide, with a fine view out over the Insh Marshes. Return to the main path and turn left along the top of a river terrace with woods of birch and aspen to the left and fields to the right. Cross a bridge over a tiny burn amid huge banks of rounded pebbles and take a small path descending left to the Invertromie Hide, down a dry valley overhung with aspens and carpeted with mosses, heather and *Cladonia* lichens. The hide at the bottom gives more intimate views of the marshes, and you may see roe deer at close quarters. Then return to the main path and turn left along the edge of the wood to a fine stand of mature aspens. Insh Marshes reserve has some of the best stands of this tree in Britain. Bear right beside the fence, then cross an open area where in summer devil's bit scabious and field gentian flower.

Map labels: Insh Marshes, Invertromie, B970, Tromie Bridge, Killighurtly, River Tromie, Woods of Glentromie, Kennels, ½ Km, ½ mile

2 At a path junction turn right to take the continuing trail through a gate into birch woodland. Cross the track leading to Invertromie Farm and wind uphill and then down through glacial deposit scenery, with many kettle holes. Turn downhill towards the River Tromie. Take the right fork at the Y-junction ignoring the path signed 'Old Churchyard' of which little now remains. Admire the wall to your left, which is carpeted with splendidly luxuriant lichens and mosses.

3 Go down steps and cross a small burn on stepping stones, then walk by the river through a delightful meadow. In summer look for fragrant and heath spotted orchids. Leave the waymarked path here and

Goldeneye

follow one nearer the water's edge (with care) to see the spectacular gorge. Then rejoin the path to go through a gate onto the road and turn left.

4   Cross Tromie Bridge and turn right along a track, signed to the Gaick and Minigaig Passes. The river foams below to your right and to your left is a mature pinewood. Go on ahead, past Killiehuntly Farm. Look for rock roses in the grass beside the track, now metalled. Descend slightly to walk beside the river again and enjoy the view up the glen to the high rounded mountains. There are planted conifers on the left and mature birches on the right; and after a while there are houses visible on the far side of the river.

5   Cross the river on a wide wooden bridge with white railings. It is signed 'Private Bridge, cross at own risk' but it is very sturdy. Walk up past 'Keeper's Cottage' and kennels on the left and climb a high stile over the deer fence on the right, following a small sign for Ruthven. Beyond, do not follow the arrow pointing left but continue straight ahead on a grassy track. At the Y-junction take the right, rather obscure track and carry on down to the river-bank. Enjoy this delightful grassy way as it winds through mature scattered birch beside the clear bubbling water. Look for dippers on the river, and goldcrests, long-tailed tits and tree creepers in the birches. You may even see black grouse if you are lucky.

6   Eventually the path moves away from the river and crosses an expanse of open moor to a gate onto the B970. Turn right and 110yds/100m further on go through a gate on the left and along a tiny path leading away from the road, with a fence to your left. Join a larger path and turn left through a gate to walk through birch woodland. Cross the Invertromie Farm track again and go through a gate to walk through the field, with first a wall and then a fence to your left, to come to a kissing gate. Pass through, turn left and retrace your steps to the car park.

Practicals

Type of walk: This ramble is all on paths, tracks and a very minor road, so it is easy going. Lovely woodlands and an exciting river.

Complete distance: 5 miles/8km
Time: 2–3 hours
Maps: OS Explorer 402/Landranger 35

6

Feshie Bridge, Loch Insh and Uath Lochans

Park in the Forestry Commission car park at Feshie Bridge, grid ref 849047. To access this, take the B970 which runs along the opposite side of the Spey Valley from the A9. It can be reached from Kingussie, Kincraig or Inverdruie near Aviemore.

Loch Insh is extensively used for kayaking, wind-surfing and sailing, but it still has plenty of wildlife. Look out particularly for ospreys fishing.

Kettlehole lochans are depressions formed at the end of the last Ice Age when blocks of ice, isolated in moraine, finally melted to leave a hole, which often filled with water. Eskers are gravel ridges formed as the beds of rivers running under the ice were left 'high and dry' when the ice melted.

The **River Feshie** is a classic example of a gravel-bed river meandering along the alluvial floodplain and dividing into many channels, which change from time to time, to create a 'braided' pattern. Then where the rock becomes harder it has cut out a narrow channel full of rapids and small falls.

1 Leave the car park by the path at the far end which slopes upward to join a pleasant moss-grown track. Turn right and walk on through woodland, then beside a field wall and into more woodland; do not take the waymarked path down the river terrace on your right. Beyond the wood is an open space with a cottage; the footpath is clearly signed, going straight ahead and into more trees. Go past another house, with Invereshie House away in the trees. At the foot of the bank go through a gate and walk straight ahead along a track, which winds round Invereshie Farm and then comes out onto a minor road near Kincraig. Turn left and follow the paved footpath, part of the Badenoch Way, along the road beside Loch Insh to the Loch Insh Watersports Centre.

Turn right and walk round the back of the main building, which houses an excellent café. Goldeneye frequent the loch all year round and may be seen with ducklings in summer.

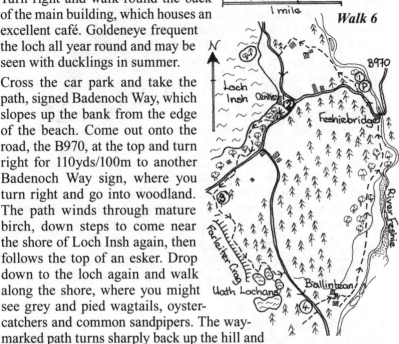

2 Cross the car park and take the path, signed Badenoch Way, which slopes up the bank from the edge of the beach. Come out onto the road, the B970, at the top and turn right for 110yds/100m to another Badenoch Way sign, where you turn right and go into woodland. The path winds through mature birch, down steps to come near the shore of Loch Insh again, then follows the top of an esker. Drop down to the loch again and walk along the shore, where you might see grey and pied wagtails, oyster-catchers and common sandpipers. The way-marked path turns sharply back up the hill and winds through trees to come out on the road opposite a cottage called 'Druimuachdar'. Cross the road, walk right for a few metres, to take a

Feshie Bridge

23

small gate on the left. The path runs along beside the road and then turns away into the wood. Climb steeply to a forest track, and turn left. Here look up high for crossbills, which might be feeding on the cones of the pines.

Crossbill

3 This track winds gently upwards round a knoll and then leaves the Badenoch Way as it goes off right. Go ahead on a track, which soon descends to cross a small valley. It brings you to the first of four Uath Lochans, which are probably kettlehole lochans. Go left at the junction and wind round a car park above the lovely secluded pools. Join the minor road up Glen Feshie, where you turn right.

4 After 330yds/300m, take a left turn into a track to Ballinteam, and follow this down to keep right at a three-way junction. Go past a square of cottages. Admire a fine sculpture of owls and squirrels on a post, and turn left in front of it to descend a path, waymarked by the Scottish Rights of Way Society. This runs down by one of the cottages. At the foot of the slope, turn right to walk along the side of a field fence to the river bank, still following waymarks. Then go left along the floodplain, with the wide braided River Feshie to your right. Cross a grassy area, with heather and devil's-bit scabious, and go on into scattered alder and birch woodland. Cross a minor burn at a ford. Beyond a gate, go over a flat area, with a quarry above on the left, and then follow the track as it climbs the bank of the river terrace to join the quarry track. Turn right and go through a gate. Carry on past a hill on the right and then suddenly you are beside the River Feshie once more. Here it is full of rapids and is very dramatic. Continue past a cottage to join the road at Feshiebridge. Turn left and, after 220yds/200m, turn right down into the car park.

Practicals

Type of walk: A delightful ramble along good paths and tracks, including a short section of the Badenoch Way.

Complete distance:	6 miles/9.5km
Time:	3 hours
Maps:	OS Explorers 402 and 403/Landranger 35

Sgor Gaoith

Park in the large car park, just outside the forest, on the left, at the end of the public road, grid ref 851984. Access this by the minor road, which leaves the B970 just east of Feshiebridge, signed to Lagganlia and Achlean. Drive along it for as far as you can.

Sgor Gaoith **(the Peak of the Winds)**, a Munro, is the highest point on the long ridge enclosing the Loch Einich glacial trough on the west. The ridge is splendidly steep and craggy on its east side above Loch Einich, but its west side above Glen Feshie is relatively gentle and rounded, giving easy routes to the top. This is the last very high ground of the Cairngorms, at the western edge of the huge granite intrusion.

Sgor Gaoith

South of Sgor Gaoith is the Moine Mhor **(the Great Moss** or **Bog)**, an extensive remote stretch of continuously high ground. It is mossier and less stony than the higher ridges to the east, so is more attractive to birds like golden plover and dotterel. In spite of this somewhat gentler aspect it can be fearsome in bad weather, especially in winter, when its featureless expanses are scoured by wind and snow. Unfortunately there are now bulldozed tracks over parts of it which detract from the sense of wildness.

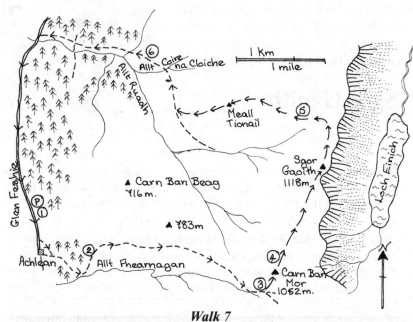

Walk 7

1 Continue on along the road towards Achlean farm. When you can see the roofs of the farm, in a hollow in front, look on the left for a sign to Carn Ban Mor painted on a rock. Follow the path indicated, across the grass and into a wood by a small gate. Where the path divides take the rising left branch through young pines, with spaces between the trees carpeted with bearberry. As you ascend the trees become sparser and eventually you emerge on the open hillside.

2 Follow the distinct, well-graded path, cross a burn (channelled) and climb gently up the side of a spur to a col. Go through a glacial melt-water notch, then up the ridge connecting the col to the massif ahead. To your right is the deep valley of the Allt Fhearnagan. Carry on along the path, which winds right, to run beside the burn, now very small. It ends at a spring in a hollow, full of moss, which holds late snow. Carry on to a large cairn and path junction on the broad watershed.

3 Ignore two obvious paths leading away from the cairn, and take an indistinct path, which leads left to the summit of Carn Ban Mor, the highest ground visible to the left. This is Cairngorm country and the vegetation is sparse and tundra-like, though grassier than on the bigger hills farther east. To the south spreads the high level mossy plateau of Am Moine Mhor. Look for dotterel and ptarmigan here, and occasionally you may see snow buntings even in summer. There is a ring cairn

on the top of Carn Ban Mor where you might like to eat your picnic in shelter.

4 Head on north to descend a little to a col, then climb again to the summit of Sgor Gaoith (3,690ft/1118m). The summit cairn is perched spectacularly above the cliffs to the west of Loch Einich, and beyond the dizzying gap towers Braeriach, the third highest mountain in Scotland. Pause here to enjoy the magnificent view. Then walk on north above the cliff edge to the next col and turn left to leave the ridge.

Bearberry

5 Carry on down over a small raise and then another lower top and down the obvious spur, Meall Tionail. There is no path but the going is pleasant and easy. Go over the edge of the spur and continue descending through heather, which is not quite so easy. Look for an obvious path contouring the hillside below and make your way down to join it and turn right. Ford a burn, the Allt Coire na Cloiche, and go on along the path into scattered mature pine trees, where you might spot crested tits.

Dotterel

6 The path here is very beautiful. It fords another burn, the Allt nam Bo, and then runs high along the side of a gorge with the river, the Allt Ruadh, far below. Stroll on along the path, which becomes a track. Go ahead at a cross of tracks, through a forest gate into planted woodland, and down to the road. Turn left and walk the 1¼ miles/2km along the road to your car.

Practicals

Type of walk: A fine climb on good paths. The descent is trackless for part of the way. There is some unavoidable road walking at the end.

Complete distance: 10 miles/16km
Time: 6–7 hours
Maps: OS Explorer 403/Landranger 35 and 36

8

Loch an Eilein from Coylumbridge

Park in the large layby before the river at Coylumbridge, grid ref 914106. Access this by the B970 to Glenmore and Cairngorm from Aviemore.

The **castle at Loch an Eilein** dates from the 14th century and was a stronghold of the Comyns, the powerful Norman family who owned Badenoch. Now it is a romantic ruin overgrown with bushes, set dramatically on its island. There are the remains of a causeway from the shore to the island but they can only be seen when the water is low.

Ospreys nested on the ruined castle for many years, but in Victorian times they were seriously persecuted. For example in 1851 a well-known egg collector, Lewis Dunbar, swam across to the castle in early May, climbed the ramparts to the nest in spite of six inches of snow, took the two eggs and swam back to shore with one in each hand. In spite of protection

*Castle,
Loch an Eilein*

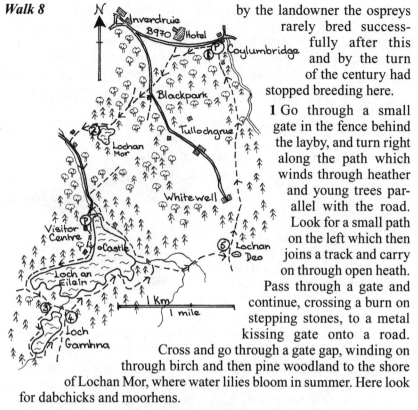

by the landowner the ospreys rarely bred success- fully after this and by the turn of the century had stopped breeding here.

1 Go through a small gate in the fence behind the layby, and turn right along the path which winds through heather and young trees par- allel with the road. Look for a small path on the left which then joins a track and carry on through open heath. Pass through a gate and continue, crossing a burn on stepping stones, to a metal kissing gate onto a road. Cross and go through a gate gap, winding on through birch and then pine woodland to the shore of Lochan Mor, where water lilies bloom in summer. Here look for dabchicks and moorhens.

2 The path then leaves the lochan and continues on through woodland. Go past two houses and out onto the minor road to Loch an Eilein. Turn left and walk up the road, with care, then turn right into the car park. Walk on past the visitor centre and shop, which you may like to visit. Head for the loch shore, walking left at the Y-junction and keeping the loch to your left. There are many small paths through the magnificent old trees but the main track is never in doubt. Quite near to the shore is the island, with its ruined castle, from which the loch gets its name. Cross a grassy area in front of a cottage and go through a gate into pine woodland, where you might spot red squirrels. At a T-junction turn left, following a waymark. The track moves into more open country with heather and scattered trees. There are good views back over the loch. You may see goosanders and goldeneye even in summer.

3 Bear right onto a small path at the end of an open area where a stand of younger pines begins. A smaller lochan, Loch Gamhna, can be seen through the trees. The path follows the shore, giving lovely views

29

across the water to the hills beyond. Go round the head of the loch, admiring the water lilies. Soon the path becomes wider, moving into open heath again. A track joins it from the right and then you arrive back at the main track, only 130yds/106m from where you left it. This extension is certainly worth doing, but if you are short of time just ignore the turn, carry on over a footbridge where the two tracks come together.

4 The track winds on round the east side of Loch an Eilein, where you may see crested tits and cross-bills. After an area of dense small pines there is a stand of tall pines on the left, with heather and scattered juniper to the right. Just before a bridge, turn right onto a track, part of the cycle network. Follow it as it leaves the mature trees and runs through heath. Cross two burns on small bridges. Ignore a sign telling cyclists to turn left and head on to a cross of tracks by a small pool, Lochan Deo.

Crested Tit

5 Turn left and follow the well-maintained path uphill through pines. Pass through two gates, to reach an open terrace, with a fine wide view over Glen More to the hills. Follow the path as it runs downhill into birch and juniper, through another gate into pines and down to the campsite at Coylumbridge. Go straight ahead down the track to the main road, where you turn left to your car.

Practicals

Type of walk: A glorious ramble through fine woodland, over open heath and beside a fine loch and several pretty lochans. Good paths and tracks. An easy, mainly level, route.

Complete distance: 8½ miles/14km if you include Loch Gamhna, or 7¼ miles/11.5km

Time: 5 hours or 4 hours

Maps: OS Explorer 403/Landranger 36

Craigellachie Nature Reserve, Aviemore

Park in the small car park on the left by the now defunct Tourist Information Office, shortly beyond the sign to Aviemore's Youth Hostel, grid ref 894119. There is also more parking in the town and to access both, take the B9152 off the A9 which by-passes Aviemore.

Aviemore has been in existence since the 17th century but growth really began in the 1800s when the settlement became a small junction on the old Highland railway. Queen Victoria visited regularly. In the 1960s it became a thriving ski resort.

The lower slopes of the hill of Craigellachie are cloaked in mature birch woodland. Scenic trails through the birchwood provide fine views across Aviemore and Strathspey to the Cairngorms. The hill used to mark the southern limit of the Grant territory. At one time the Grants owned all the land between the Upper and Lower Craigellachies and their war cry was **'Stand fast, Craigellachie'**.

1 Walk back south along the B-road and turn right towards the Youth Hostel, also signed to the Catholic Church and the Nature Reserve (NR). Keep to the right beside a tall hedge, then go downhill to enter the NR by an underpass below the A9. The path curves round into

Least Water Lily

very pleasant birchwoods below the spectacular crag of Craigellachie. Look for peregrine falcons circling round. You may also see slowworms on the path.

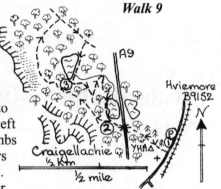

Walk 9

2 Keep left at the first junction to climb the stepped path, then left again at the next. This path climbs steeply at first but then contours the hillside below the crags. There are fine views out over

Craigellachie

Aviemore to Glen More and the Cairngorms. After a while the path descends slightly to join a track. Turn right and go downhill, then at the next junction turn right again. Soon the path comes to an artificial lochan and runs along the low dam wall. Mallards feed among the pond-weed and dabchicks hide in the sedges; dragonflies patrol the fringes of the lochan in summer.

Dabchick

3 Bear left at the far side of the lochan, following a waymark, and wander downhill through the lovely birch woodland, where beech fern and hard fern thrive. Turn left at the T-junction, following the good path, which makes an acute-angled bend, then runs beside a fence beyond which is the A9. The way zigzags down to another small lochan with mallards and dragonflies and large patches of the yellow least waterlily. Walk round the shore and up the far side to rejoin your outward path near the entrance tunnel.

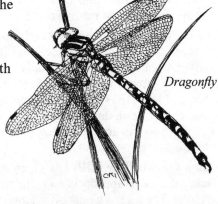

Dragonfly

Practicals

Type of walk: A delightful ramble through birchwood beneath the crags of Craigellachie.

Complete distance:	1½ miles/2.5km
Time:	1–2 hours
Maps:	OS Explorer 403/Landranger 35 or 36

10

Cairn Lochan and Cairn Gorm

Park in the enormous car park where the road ends half way up the mountain, grid ref 989062. To access this, take the minor road to Glenmore and Cairngorm from Aviemore. It starts off as the B970 but is unclassified beyond Coylumbridge.

Cairn Gorm (4103ft/1244m) is the sixth highest mountain in Britain. It is situated right on the edge of the plateau overlooking Glen More and Speyside. Because of the ski road up into Coire Cas it is very easy of access and the climb starts high (about 1956ft/620m); it is extremely popular, but needs to be treated with respect. Coire Cas is disfigured with ski tows and a funicular railway, but the other northern corries are unspoilt and magnificent.

The railway was built only recently, after much controversy. There were worries about inexperienced and improperly equipped people wandering around on the plateau, and also about the damage that could be caused by crowds to the fragile upland habitat. As a result of this you may not leave the café at the terminus to go out onto the hill, nor may you catch a train down at the end of your walk. We are, however, assured that you can go in for a bowl of soup as long as you leave your rucksack outside.

Cairn Gorm (Blue Hill) has given its name to the whole range, replacing the more appropriate Gaelic name of Am Monadh Ruadh (Red Hills). The rock is a pinkish granite, which weathers to give poor acid soils and stony tundra. It has been gouged by the action of glaciers, producing splendid corries and two great passes which cut right through the massif, the most noticeable being the Lairig Ghru, visible in all the views from Speyside.

1   Walk up towards the terminal for the railway and the chair lift and just before them take a path, right, which descends steps to cross a burn. Follow it as it contours round the hillside, leading away from all the ski tows and associated paraphernalia. Keep on along the path, taking the

right branch at the Y- junction below Coire an t-Sneachda. Cross the burn and again take the right branch below Coire an Lochain. Harebells, thyme and heather grow by the path, and look for cloudberry flowers and berries in summer.

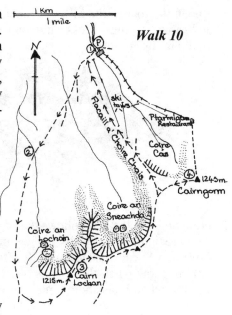

Walk 10

2 Cross the burn from Coire an Lochain. The path bends left and begins a long gradual ascent up the side of the spur, which encloses the corrie on the west. After ½ mile/1km the path reaches a plateau where a burn rises in a wet area. Most of the ground, however, is dry, stony and tundra-like and walking is very easy. Carry on across the level area until you are well past the cliffs at the head of Coire an Lochain. Then turn left off the main path, which carries on to Ben Macdui, and climb steeper ground to the summit of Cairn Lochan. You are likely to see ptarmigan scuttling

Coire an Lochain

among the rocks, like little speckled hens; there may also be dotterel and snow buntings. Moss campion flowers on the stony ground until well into the summer.

Moss Campion

3 From now on, the way follows the edge of the northern corries, above their precipitous headwalls and the impressive jagged ridge of Fiacaill Coire an t-Sneachda. Go carefully if the visibility is poor, and particularly in snow when the edge is often corniced. The path down from Cairn Lochan joins another more obvious path at a bealach. Turn left and carry on over the high point above Coire an t-Sneachda and down to another bealach, then go gently uphill again to the top of a slight raise. Note the path going left here along Fiacaill a'Choire Chais, this is your way down, but unless the weather has closed in, bear right (east) round the head of Coire Cas and up the bouldery slopes to the summit of Cairn Gorm. There is a large cairn and a weather station here, and the Ptarmigan Restaurant a short distance down from the top. The views are superb.

4 When you are ready to leave retrace your steps west to the raise at the start of Fiacaill a'Choire Chais, and turn right (north) on a path down this ridge. When the path swings off to the right to go down to join a track among the ski tows, leave it and continue along the crest of the ridge. The walking is very easy over open stony ground with scattered low vegetation. As you get lower you may have to avoid some snow fences, but most of these and the ski tows are to your right. Finally you reach your outward path. Turn right and return to the car park.

Ptarmigan

Practicals

Type of walk: A fine climb that is not too steep but gives excellent views into the northern corries of the Cairngorm Massif. Because Cairn Lochan is a Top, not a full Munro, it is much less frequented than Cairn Gorm and Ben Macdui, so it is less worn and you are more likely to meet wildlife. The paths are mostly good and walking is easy, but you must always bear in mind that much of the Cairngorm plateau is above 3500ft/1100m. This means that it is much colder than in the valley and the winds will be much more severe. Paths are not always clear on the stony ground, and in mist there are few landmarks. In snow stay well away from the corrie edges, which are often corniced. If the weather changes your best advice would be to go down immediately by the route of ascent or by Fiacaill a'Choire Chais, depending where you are. Bear in mind that accidents have occurred here.

Complete distance:	8 miles/13km.
Time:	6 hours
Maps:	OS Explorer 403/Landranger 36

Rock Roses

11

The Chalamain Gap and Creag a' Chalamain

Park in Allt Mor car park, on the left of the road, about ½ mile/1km beyond the Visitor Centre at Glenmore, grid ref 983087. Access this by the road to Glenmore from Aviemore.

The **Chalamain Gap**, which cuts through a spur and forms a convenient route from Glen More to the Lairig Ghru, is one of the best known glacial meltwater channels. These steep-sided notches were cut by powerful rivers, running below the ice, as the glaciers retreated. Their orientation was determined by the ice and so often bears no relation to normal river courses, frequently cutting across hillsides or spurs instead.

Reindeer were probably native in Scotland until the 12th century. Occasional attempts to reintroduce them failed until, in 1954, some reindeer were brought from Sweden by a Lapp, Mikel Utsi. The reindeer took a long time to become established but then did well in the pine forest, south of Loch Morlich. They now roam free over the Cairngorm plateau, feeding mainly on lichens. All the animals now present are Scottish born and bred.

Reindeer

Sgar Gaoith from Creag a' Chalamain

Walk 11

1 Leave the car park at the far end and cross the Allt Mor on a curved wooden footbridge. Turn right to walk up beside the burn on the well-made Allt Mor trail to the road. Creeping lady's tresses and oak fern grow among bilberry under the pines. Go over the road, with care, and carry on by the burn, crossing side burns on bridges, until you reach a bridge over the Allt Mor at a cross of paths.

2 Turn right, cross the bridge and go steeply up steps on the far side. The path turns right, levels out and runs high above the burn, then winds round left and follows the edge of the valley. Look for reindeer in the enclosures to your right. Keep on along the distinct gravel path, which turns right and runs above the river, with a splendid view across to the

39

corries on the north side of the Cairngorm massif. After ½ mile/1km the path descends to a burn. Cross on stepping-stones and continue up the main path heading for the Chalamain Gap.

3 Go up the well-made path into the Gap. At the top, follow the path as it winds between a mass of large boulders. In some places you will have to scramble over them. At the far side are a number of small pools. Look on your right for a path up the hillside and follow it to the craggy top of Creag a' Chalamain, 2566ft/787m. The views are superb, back to Cairngorm and ahead to Braeriach, with Sgor Gaoith to its right, then out across Glen More.

4 From the summit cairn go ahead down a small path, which soon disappears, but carry on to cross a col and ascend very easily up the far side to the rounded summit of Castle Hill.

5 Make your way, half-right, down the trackless, fairly easy side of the hill, keeping well to the left to avoid deep valleys. Go on down the final steepish descent, through long heather, to the east end of Eag a'Chait, which you cross. Climb up the far side to the deer fence and walk along beside it to take a gate and stile (both slightly awkward to negotiate at present) and then continue on a path along the shore of a small lochan. Go on round the lower slopes of Airgiod-meall and descend quite steeply to enter the pinewood. Carry on down through the trees where the path soon becomes drier and easier to follow. Go past a hut, then cross a bog to reach a track beside a deer fence. Turn right to go through a gate in the fence, and follow the good track on down the valley. Watch out for spotted flycatchers and crested tits.

6 At the next track junction turn right and then left at the one after that. Keep on along the obvious track until it comes down gradually to the road. Turn left, cross and walk along the track into the car park.

Practicals

Type of walk: Mostly on good paths and forest tracks. There is a trackless area from Castle Hill down to the end of Eag a'Chait and the continuing path is unsurfaced and can be wet until well into the forest.

Complete distance:	7 miles/11.5km
Time:	5 hours
Maps:	OS Explorer 403/Landranger 36

Sluggan Bridge

Park in a small car park, on the left of a minor road, where it crosses a track, one of General Wade's Military roads, grid ref 875213. Access this by travelling 3 miles/5km along the road, which leaves the B9153 in Carrbridge just immediately south of the River Dulnain.

Sluggan Bridge, constructed around 1729, lies on one of the many roads built by General Wade. At first the road crossed the River Dulnain by a ford, but the river comes up fast after rain and so a two-arched bridge was built. In August 1829 this was swept away in the great flood, and the present bridge with a large single span was built to replace it. Recently the bridge has been extensively repaired by Sustrans as part of the National Cycle Network, and railings have been installed along the sides of the bridge. Previously there were no parapets, which could be quite alarming with children as the bridge is very high.

Sluggan Bridge

C.M.Isherwood

Tinder, hoof or razor-strop fungus grows on many of the old birch trees. It forms large brackets, which are hoof shaped, hard and woody, with grey concentric patterns and grooves on its upper surface. It could be used to sharpen razors because of its hardness, and also for tinder, hence its names.

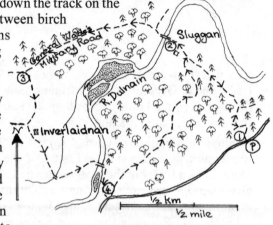

Walk 12

1 Cross the road and go down the track on the far side. It zigzags between birch and pine, and joins another track coming in on the right. Head on down to the bottom of the shallow valley and continue along the level between large pines, with a bog on the left and a sandy hill, much tunnelled by rabbits, on the right. Walk on between enormous larches into an open grassy area, the in-bye of the cottage at East Sluggan, now unfortunately a ruin. Carry on past the cottage and down to the River Dulnain, where you may wish to pause for a snack, or to paddle if you have children with you. The river is quite shallow and safe unless it is in spate; it does rise very quickly after rain because it drains a large mountainous catchment. Upstream it can be seen emerging from a pine and birch clad gorge, but the most dramatic feature is the splendid bridge, on which the track crosses. It is much more complete than the better known similar one at Carrbridge, with all the roadway remaining as well as the arch. Look on the sandbanks for otter footprints.

2 When you are ready to leave this delightful corner, cross the gated bridge and walk on along the path, away from the river, into a valley among pine and birch. Many of the birches have the big grey razor-strop fungus growing on them. Watch for redstarts and spotted flycatchers in summer. The path used to be grassy as it curved up the side of the valley but a new hard surfaced cycle track has now been put in.

Redstart

The way carries on along the hillside through scattered juniper, with a good view out over the Dulnain valley. It then comes close beside a fenced plantation, on the right, as it dips down to cross a tiny burn.

3 Beyond, take an indistinct path, left, very boggy at first, but soon improving, as it crosses a rough field. It then becomes a track leading to Inverlaidnan Farm. Here, turn left on a wider track past the farm buildings and the large house. Continue on across the floodplain of the river. There are large clumps of field gentian in the grass, with harebells and devil's-bit scabious. Cross the Dulnain on a substantial wooden bridge and follow the track right through a quarried area beside the river.

4 Climb uphill on the road, now metalled, before leaving it for a grassy track, on the left, closed off to traffic by a single barrier. Continue along this lovely way, winding through small grassy hills and valleys with scattered birch and juniper. Gradually the trees become closer and the path a stony track through a wood. Pass through a gateway and stride, uphill, to an open grassy area on a hilltop, surrounded by forest. Walk straight ahead and on into the trees at the far side. Look for chickweed wintergreen in the grass beneath the pines. The path bends round to the right and then swings left, making a long descent to come out at the foot of a grassy slope, dotted with mountain pansies in summer, just across the pasture from East Sluggan. Cross the grass on your right and rejoin your outward track to return to your car.

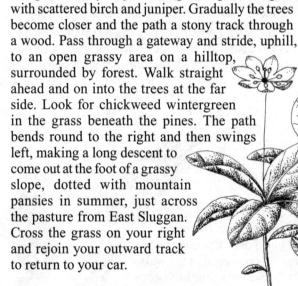

Chickweed Wintergreen

Practicals

Type of walk: A delightful easy ramble on paths and tracks, with only a couple of wet areas to negotiate.

Complete distance: 3 miles/5km
Time: 2 hours
Maps: OS Explorer 403/Landranger 36

13

Loch Garten and Loch Mallachie

Park in the large car park for the osprey hide, grid ref 978184. Access this from the B970 between Boat of Garten and Nethy Bridge, crossing the Spey at Boat of Garten and following the minor road to its junction with the B970. Turn left. Take the next minor road on the right.

Loch Garten is famous for where the ospreys returned to nest after an absence of over 50 years. At first they tried to nest on the south side of the loch but failed for various reasons, not least because they were still being persecuted by egg collectors. When they transferred to their present site, north of the loch, the RSPB set up a round-the-clock watch on the nest and at last they reared young. The decision was made to let the public view the nest from a hide and this has been hugely successful. Now there are more than 100 pairs nesting in Scotland.

Osprey

The **osprey** is a magnificent bird with a 5ft/1.2m wingspan, mostly brown with a white head and a dark stripe through its eye. You may see it on several of the walks described in this book, hovering high above rivers and lochs as it looks for fish. If you are very lucky you may see it plunge into the water, feet first, and come out carrying a fish which it then carries off. Ospreys winter in Africa and return to Scotland in April.

1 First, if the ospreys are in residence, go along the well-made track to the Osprey Hide, then return to the car park. Walk back along the road, which here keeps close to the shore of Loch Garten. There are sandy

Loch Garten

beaches beneath huge old pine trees and a lovely view across the loch to Meall a'Buachaille. Where the road leaves the loch side look on the left for a small path winding through juniper and bilberry bushes, and follow it to the shore again. This is not a formal path but is a delight to walk as it meanders along above the water. Cross a bay where there are foundations of an old boathouse and carry on at the far side. Listen for common sandpipers by the water, and for goldcrests and coal tits in the trees. You may also hear the curious purring trill of crested tits. Red squirrels are common all through the woods. Look for the inconspicuous white spikes of the orchid, creeping lady's tresses, which is characteristic of these pine woods, and also the medium wintergreen.

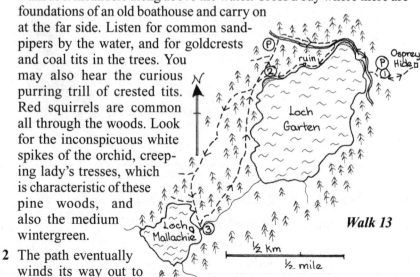

2 The path eventually winds its way out to

45

another sandy beach. Walk away from the loch for 22yds/20m on one of the many paths through the heather and bilberry, to join a wide track. Turn left and then take a right fork at the Y-junction. This pleasant sandy track wanders through pine trees and then comes out into a rather more open area where you might see roe deer. Then it goes back into a stand of very tall pines, joins another track and runs along the shore of Loch Mallachie. This is on the very edge of Abernethy Forest, with its far bank giving onto open country. There are nest boxes for goldeneye on trees round the loch and also on a small island near the path.

3   Turn left before a wide burn enters the loch, along an indistinct path which soon becomes obvious. Head on with the burn and a wide bog to the right and tall pines on a bank to the left. The burn meanders off into the end of Loch Garten, visible through the trees. Carry on up the track, past the junction taken on your outward route and past the beach to a car park in the trees and then on to join the road. Cross and walk a few steps through the heather to join a good path on the far side. Turn right and walk, with care, back to the main car park.

Creeping Lady's Tresses

Practicals

Type of walk: A very pleasant easy ramble on paths and tracks.

Complete distance: 2 miles/3.5km.
Time: As much as you have
Maps: OS Explorer 403/Landranger 36

The Braes of Abernethy and Ryvoan Pass (Linear walk)

For the northern start of this linear walk, park at grid ref 012193. Access this from the south side of the bridge in Nethy Bridge by going east, up Dell Road, for about ½ mile/1km to the entrance to the National Nature Reserve. Drive on along the track for 110yds/100m to a small parking area on the right. For the southern start of the walk, there is limited parking at the end of the Glenmore Lodge road, grid ref 989096. At the time of writing it looks as if another small car park is under construction 110yds/100m further on along the track. If these spaces are full you will have to return to the main road to the Reindeer Centre car park. To access these parking areas, take the road from Aviemore to Glenmore, turning left past the Visitor Centre and Reindeer Centre to Glenmore Lodge.

Cairn Gorm from the Braes of Abernethy

Abernethy Forest is one of the largest remaining areas of the Caledonian pine forest, home to many of the special birds, mammals and plants associated with the forest. It is an RSPB reserve and a National Nature Reserve. Many of the trees along the Braes of Abernethy are superb ancient specimens, huge and twisted, mixed in with young regenerating trees.

Black Grouse

The **RSPB** found that the deer fences round the forest were causing the deaths of many capercaillie and black grouse, which flew into them. They have removed the fences and control deer numbers by culling, necessary so that the trees will regenerate and survive. As a result the numbers of **capercaillie and blackcock** have increased.

The path is an old right of way, leading to Glenmore and from there to the west, but also to the Lairig an Laoigh, a deep trench cut through the Cairngorm massif by ice. This pass goes through to Deeside. Cattle used to be taken this way (hence the name, Pass of the Calves); it is a longer but lower route than the more obvious Lairig Ghru.

1 From the Nethy Bridge end of the walk, carry on along the track, which is the continuation of the Dell Road. At the first main track junction turn left and climb a short way up onto a ridge, where the way levels out and bears right, joining a fainter track. Ignore a track that joins from the left and go on until you can descend into an open grassy area with fields. There is another track junction here; take the right branch and go uphill to Forest Lodge. Keep right, ignoring all the tracks, which go to the lodge (used for RSPB staff and volunteers), and go past two cottages on the right to reach a forest road.

2 Cross and walk right for a very short way, to take a path on the left, through a fence opening, a Scottish Rights of Way to Glenmore and Braemar. Almost immediately take the left path at a fork and wind round to the edge of the river. The pinewood here is magnificent, with huge old trees mixed in with younger ones and juniper to give a lovely varied pattern, especially with the sun shining through the branches.

Through open spaces there is a fine view across the valley of the Nethy to Bynack More and then Cairn Gorm, which looks very dramatic from this angle.

3 Capercaillie can be found in the woods. Listen for their weird popping call, and as you come up to the edge of the woodland look for blackcock. Another track comes in from the left; wind right and climb a little, then ignore a path going right, up to an old croft, Rynettin, which you can see surrounded by fields on the hillside above. Soon the open area ends and you are back in forest. The path goes up and down into small valleys, then climbs to the unfenced forest edge. Go straight out onto high heather moorland with the bulk of Meall a'Bhuachaille to your right. Cairn Gorm can be seen to your left through the gap of the Ryvoan Pass and then Bynack Mor left again. There are two small lochans beside the track, and then the isolated Ryvoan Bothy on the right. From here it is mostly down hill.

4 Go past the track to Lairig an Laoigh and Braemar, and then up slightly to walk on a track above An Lochan Uaine, the Green Lochan, an amazing deep blue-green. Legend has it that the fairies do their washing here which gives it the colour but it is probably just deep water over mica sand. If the water is not too high there is a beach and it is a lovely place to stop for a pause, although to avoid erosion of the banks you now have to go down steps at the south end of the lochan.

5 Here join a remade track

49

suitable for bicycles and maybe even wheelchairs, which runs down the valley between Meall a'Bhuachaille and Creag nan Gall beneath huge old pines and birches. The path is very even but quite hard on the feet at the end of a long walk. Ignore a left turn (where there is a seat for only one person) then cross a burn and go uphill a little to reach the road end just by Glenmore Lodge. If you had to park down by the main road there is a path just above this road, which gives easier walking.

Medium Wintergreen

Practicals

Type of walk: Entirely on good paths and tracks along an ancient right of way through the hills, but you need to arrange transport for both ends.

Complete distance:	One way 8 miles/13km.
	There and back 16 miles/26km
Time:	4 or 8 hours
Maps:	OS Explorer 403/Landranger36

NB Glenmore Lodge has a bar, which serves drinks and food in the evening, from 5pm. It is plain food for hungry mountaineers, but is most welcome at the end of the day.

15

Nethy Bridge and Broomhill

Park outside the Nethybridge Community Hall on the Dell Road, grid ref 002204 or in the small car park at the entry to the old railway line, now the Speyside Way, if the first one is full, grid ref 001207. Access these by the B970 which runs through Nethy Bridge, or along the A95, then the minor road past Broomhill Station on the Strathspey Railway and on to Nethy Bridge. Turn up by the shop on the south side of the bridge onto the Dell Road.

Broomhill Bridge is a fine example of the wooden bridges in use at the time it was built; it was opened for traffic in 1894. Few of these

Broomhill Bridge

bridges remain. It is a listed structure and was partially reconstructed in the original style in 1987.

Drumlins are egg-shaped humps/hills, which consist of sand and gravel deposited by ice-sheets during the last glaciation.

Before the **Spey was bridged** there were ferries in many places, and these are sometimes recorded in the place names; for example Boat of Balliefurth which is approached on this walk, and Boat of Garten further upstream.

1 Return along the road to the bridge, cross and take the first left. At the entrance to the waterworks, turn left off the road, following a sign to Broomhill. The path goes between the waterboard fence and the River Nethy along the edge of an overflow channel, which it eventually crosses and re-crosses. This will not be possible if the river is high and you will have to go back to the road and walk along it. Go on through a wooded area, along an embankment behind a farm, and out into pleasant open alder woodland with the Nethy tumbling alongside. When you emerge from the trees the Nethy has joined the much wider and deeper Spey Look for otter footprints, and maybe the animals themselves, on the sandy banks. Follow the path, half right, as it moves away from the seriously undercut bank. Cross a deep ditch on a bridge and climb two stiles, onto the road by Broomhill Bridge. Cross the road, go through a gate on the far side and back down to the riverbank.

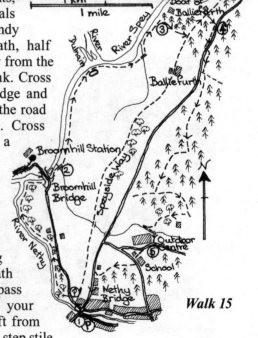

Walk 15

2 Take the footbridge over a tributary burn and carry on by the river, along a rather indistinct path that floods at times, to pass a fishermen's hut. To your right are drumlins, left from the last ice age. Cross a step stile

and continue along the top of the embankment where the path is more distinct. The fields to your right flood sometimes and often have pools, which are frequented by lapwings and oystercatchers. Teal, wigeon, mallard and goldeneye may be seen on the river, which here is broad and smooth. The embankment continues beyond the next stile, but then is closed off by a fence; bear left here, round the riverside of a small pool and reach the bank opposite the confluence with the River Dulnain. Cross a gated footbridge over a deep ditch and bear left back to the river. Go in front of another fishing hut and over a sturdy stile, beyond which the path runs along the field edge and then on top of the embankment again.

Wigeon

3 Ignore a stile on the left and cross the fence at the top of the embankment where there is no barbed wire. Turn right to walk along the edge of a wood (private), crossing a boggy ditch with care, then up a bank to a gate onto the old railway line, now the Speyside Way. Turn left and walk through pleasant pine woodland. Pass under a bridge and 70ft/20m beyond, turn right at a signpost directing you up to a small path that climbs an embankment. Follow the path through a kissing gate onto the access road to Boat of Balliefurth and turn left.

4 At the main road turn right through a small gate onto a fenced path which runs beside it. Cross with care at the crossing point and continue along the far side. Go over a track to another signpost and carry straight on for Nethy Bridge. The delightful mossy track winds through the forest, climbing steadily, with glimpses through the trees of the wide strath and distant hills. At a brown arrow waymark, turn right downhill and then wind left again along a terrace. Turn left at the next junction and climb again. On reaching the next waymark post, turn right downhill through open forest, with houses beyond a wall to your left.

Go through a gate and on along the fenced edge of a field. Turn right at the bottom to walk a grassy path to a gate. Beyond, turn left, cross a gated bridge over a burn and join an access road, which you follow right to a public road.

5 Turn right and walk along the road with care. Ignore a gate on the left with a brown arrow waymark. Instead turn left at the end of the fence, a few metres further on, along a fenced path which crosses a ditch on a plank bridge and then runs beside a school playing field. Go between buildings at the far side to come out onto another road. Turn left and cross to go through a derelict kissing gate into a pine wood. Walk beside the fence between the wood and the golf course, and turn right at a fence corner. There is a whole network of paths here and you can more or less choose your own, but keep the golf course in view to your right. When you can see the clubhouse, and a grey house, ahead through the trees, take a small gate onto the golf course. Cut across a corner to another gate onto the golf course car park. The golf club serves refreshments to the general public. Walk down the access road to the main road and turn left. Go along the verge, in front of the Nethy Bridge Hotel, then over the bridge and turn left to return to where you have parked.

Practicals

Type of walk: Pleasant and varied, mostly on unsurfaced paths. The way through the wood is waymarked (brown arrows) as far as the first road in Nethy Bridge. After heavy or prolonged rain parts of the river path will be inaccessible. Save the walk for when the rivers are not in spate.

Complete distance: 7 miles/11.5km
Time: 4 hours.
Maps: OS Explorer 419/Landranger 36

Anagach Woods, Grantown-on-Spey

Park in the small car park in Anagach Woods at the start of the walk, grid ref 035274. Otherwise there is ample parking in Grantown Square, grid ref 033278, or on the main street. To access these, turn off the A95, down Speyside, onto the A939, which goes through the centre of the Grantown. To reach the Anagach Woods car park, turn right at the south-east corner of the Square and drive to the end of the road.

Curling is similar to bowls. Two teams, of four each, play on a well prepared rectangular sheet of ice. The aim of the game is to slide polished granite stones along the ice towards a target, called 'house'.

Old Spey Bridge

Two sweepers with brooms help direct the stones to their resting place. Curling was played in Scotland as early as the 16th century. Then, it would have taken place on an old pond. At first flat-bottomed river stones or heavy stone weights from weavers' beams were used.

Grantown-on-Spey is an early example of a Georgian planned town, designed and built in 1760s by Sir James Grant to house the people away from the gates of Castle Grant. He also built factories and other facilities.

1 Walk down Forest Road, leaving Grantown Square at the south-east corner, signed 'Speyside Way and Anagach Forest Walks'. Cross Woodside Avenue and continue past the golf course to the small car park at the entry to Anagach Woods. Go left on the Speyside Way, past the information boards, along a track on the woodland edge. At a cross of tracks go slightly left, ignoring two turns on the right and following both Speyside Way signs and red waymarkers. Walk past a small building and a curling pond on the left. Then bear left along the edge of a clearing into mature pine forest. When the golf course clubhouse comes into view, on the left, bear right following the red waymarkers.

2 At the next junction bear left to pass through a cleared area into more mature forest, part of a capercaillie

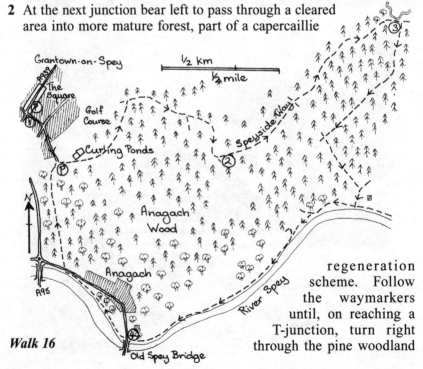

Walk 16

regeneration scheme. Follow the waymarkers until, on reaching a T-junction, turn right through the pine woodland to the edge of the trees, with fields beyond a fence, and a burn curving away.

3 At a path junction turn right, still following the red waymarkers, which lead back into the trees. Turn left at a cross of tracks. Walk round a barrier to join another track and follow it, right, until it joins yet another high above the River Spey. A few metres beyond the junction, where the main track swings right, look for a small path on the left. Follow this along the top of the riverbank, then gently down through the trees, until you can join another track below a wooden house. At first the river is almost obscured by trees but soon these open out to give good views. Look for herons on the rocks, and mallards and oystercatchers.

4 At the Old Spey Bridge, which is interestingly asymmetrical with three arches of diminishing height, go up the steps. Enjoy the views of the river from the top, then go down the far side and along a path

Capercaillie

beside the water with grassland to the right. Round a bend in the lovely waterway, go past a fishermen's hut and into trees. At the far side of the wood there is a bench on the bank. Here climb wooden steps on the right and cross the road. Walk straight ahead, go round a barrier and on up a long sandy track which once was an old military road. It runs through pines at first, with a mix of beech as it gets further from the river, and is a wonderful sight in autumn. Ignore the many paths going off on both sides. Wind slightly right and go round a gate to reach the Anagach Woods car park or retrace your steps into the town.

Practicals

Type of walk: This level ramble on good tracks and sandy paths is dry underfoot except after heavy rain. The pinewood contrasts pleasingly with the more open country of the riverbank.

Complete distance:	5½ miles/9km
Time:	3 hours
Maps:	OS Explorer 419/Landranger 36

17

Glen Brown and Glen A'an (Avon)

Park in a large layby on the east side of the main road going down to Bridge of A'an (Avon), grid ref 149202, or in a picnic area with parking for two or three cars on the other side of the river off the B9136. The two are connected by the Old Bridge of A'an and by a short footpath. Access this by the A939 from Grantown to Tomintoul.

Lapwings or Green Plovers are found throughout the British Isles. In winter the numbers are greatly increased by immigrants from Europe. The erect crest, round wings, and black and white dress are easily recognised, but the lapwing is not really black and white, but has a beautiful glossy green back, with rich chestnut patches above and below the tail. In flight it really does 'lap' its wings, giving it its name. The birds haunt marshy fields and rough upland pastures but are also found on tidal flats. They are useful birds, destroying unhelpful insects in the soil.

Juniper is readily identified by its sharp pointed needles, standing out from the stem in groups of three, and

Lapwing

by its pleasantly aromatic odour. Its black berries develop from minute green female flowers and in their first autumn are greenish–blue in colour, not ripening fully until their second year. They are used for flavouring gin.

1 From the layby go up to the main road. Cross with care and continue along a metalled driveway with a Scottish Rights of Way Sign to Dorback and a blue waymarker. In 110yds/100m keep right on a re-inforced track through mature coniferous woodland. Walk on until you reach a moss-lined path on the right, reached by crossing a small bridge over a ditch and go on. The way winds up through trees to a stile

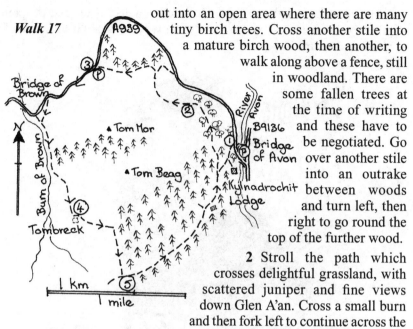

Walk 17

out into an open area where there are many tiny birch trees. Cross another stile into a mature birch wood, then another, to walk along above a fence, still in woodland. There are some fallen trees at the time of writing and these have to be negotiated. Go over another stile into an outrake between woods and turn left, then right to go round the top of the further wood.

2 Stroll the path which crosses delightful grassland, with scattered juniper and fine views down Glen A'an. Cross a small burn and then fork left to continue across the waymarked pasture, passing between electricity pylons. Towards the far side of the pasture the path joins an old sunken track, where you turn left and walk up alongside a forest fence. Beyond the brow of the hill the path comes down to a car park at White Bridge.

3 Here you have some unavoidable road walking. Cross the road and turn left, using the wide verge. The views down towards Bridge of Brown and beyond are very pleasant. As you descend, the road makes a wide hairpin with a barrier on the left; cross and take a small path down behind the barrier, which leads to a track beside the Burn of Brown. Turn left and walk along this sometimes wet track, enjoying the lovely burn. Go through a dense conifer wood for a short way, then out into open pasture with juniper.

4 Turn left at a ruined cottage and climb more steeply on an indistinct grassy path. Glen Brown is spread out before you, with many ruined crofts. There are curlews and lapwings, and the grass is full of flowers including mountain pansies and rockroses. At the top of the hill turn right on another track running along the side of a plantation. Go through a gate gap and downhill to join a reinforced track in the valley.

5 Turn left to go through a gate and along the forestry track. Look out for siskins and crossbills feeding in the trees. Keep to the main track,

59

ignoring turns to left and right. Go through a deer gate, past the path where you turned off on your outward way, and down to the road. Cross and return to your car.

Old Bridge of A'an

Practicals

Type of walk: Undulating, mostly on good paths or tracks. Some road walking. Pleasant views.

Complete distance: 4½ miles/7.5km
Time: 2–3 hours
Maps: OS Explorer 404/Landranger 36

18

Scalan and Tom Trumper

Park in Eskemulloch car park at the end of the public road, grid ref 245204. To access this, take the B9008 north from Tomintoul and, after 4 miles/7km, turn right on a minor road signed to Chapeltown and the College of Scalan. At a fork take the left branch.

Scalan, a small 18th century stone-built house, in the Braes of Glenlivet, has always been important in the history of Scotland's Catholic Church. Here boys, intending to become priests began their education or completed their courses for the priesthood, keeping the faith alive in northern Scotland. From 1716 to 1799 one hundred priests were trained in this little seminary.

Scalan

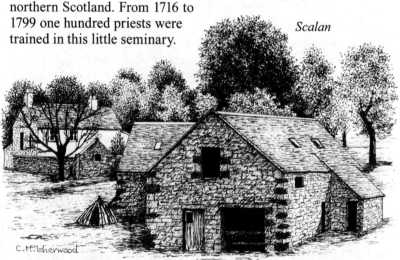

Hanoverian soldiers raided Scalan in 1726 and 1728, and burned it down after Culloden. In 1767 the rector, John Geddes, the future Bishop Geddes, erected a new building of lime and stone and this is the main part of the house you see early on this walk.

1 Carry on along the track following the Scottish Rights of Way sign and a blue Glenlivet 'walk 2' sign. The track passes between pastures, goes by a wood, and then continues over fields. In spring and early summer the verges are bright with flowers, especially mountain pansies in a variety of colours. Lapwings call and curlews bubble, and there are redshanks, oystercatchers and skylarks. Go through a small gate and wind round to the right to see the little cluster of buildings, at Scalan, come into view. Continue on to cross the bridge over the Crombie Water to the seminary building, which is being restored and is always open. There are two old mills which you cannot enter, and a spring called the Bishop's Well. Across the burn is all that remains of the first seminary.

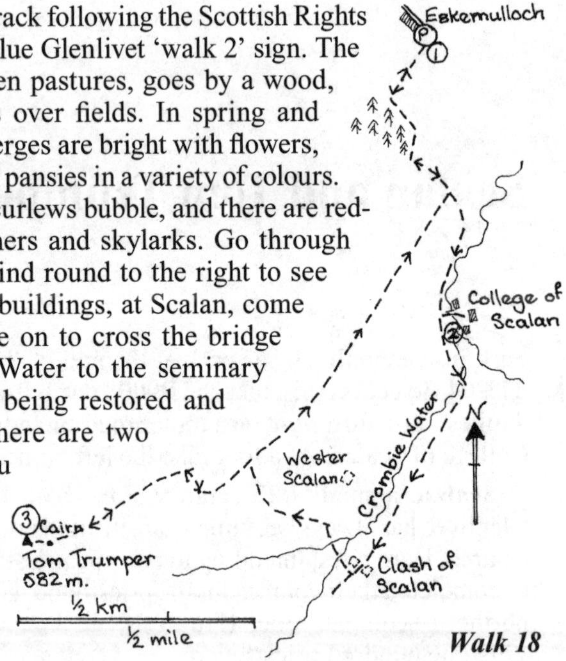

Map labels: Eskemulloch · College of Scalan · Crombie Water · Wester Scalan · Clash of Scalan · ③ Cairn · Tom Trumper 582 m. · ½ km · ½ mile · N · **Walk 18**

2 Return over the bridge and walk a grassy path up the glen. Cross a second bridge over the burn and press on along the far side until you reach a ruined farmhouse, the Clash of Scalan. Follow the waymark directing you, right, down to ford the burn and then go up the far side and across the pasture to a large larch tree beside a low ruined wall. Turn left and walk beside it until it peters out, then wind right and up to the corner of the pasture. Cross two stiles and head diagonally left, up the hill by the zigzagging path, mainly through grassland with pansies, milkwort, tormentil, and some scattered heather and bilberry. Listen for golden plovers and look for their sharp-winged silhouettes as they fly over. The grassy way joins a track running up beside grouse butts to a cairn. To reach the summit of Tom Trumper, head on for just a few metres to enjoy the splendid view which awaits of Ben A'an and Beinn a'Bhuird, with other Cairngorms behind to the south. To the north you can see Ben Rinnes and, to the east, the Ladder Hills.

Golden Plover

3 Return by your outward path as far as the double stile. Cross the first one, then walk down the field with the fence to your right and a fine view ahead. Cross the next stile and descend the flowery pasture, with the buildings of Scalan nestling in their hollow below to the right. The stile at the end of the field brings you out onto the approach track, where you turn left and return to the car park.

Mountain Pansy

Practicals

Type of walk: A very pleasant walk with good paths

Total distance:	4 miles/6.5km
Time:	3 hours
Maps:	OS Explorer 404/Landranger 36

NB During the shooting season, from August 12th, you are asked just to walk the loop and not to climb Tom Trumper.

19

Carn Daimh from Tomnavoulin

Park in Clash Wood car park just outside Tomnavoulin, grid ref 207266. To access this take the B9008 from Tomintoul along Glen Livet. Turn left onto a minor road just beyond Tomnavoulin, which is signed to the Clash Wood car park.

Petty Whin is a prickly, shrubby plant, with bright yellow blossoms, like a very small broom, that grows freely on moors and heaths. The slender branches spread in all directions and are covered with spines and tiny lance-shaped leaves. It grow to about two feet in height and flowers through May and June.

This walk follows part of the **Robbie MacPherson Smugglers Trail**. MacPherson's whisky became some of the most sought after in the land. It was taken out of the glen by packhorse carrying casks of the outlawed spirit, using lonely secret paths unknown to the excisemen.

Ladder Hills from Clash Wood

During the winter, when the trails were often impassable, MacPherson would store his whisky in holes in the hillside.

1 From the car park, walk through the barrier and up the forest track for 110yds/100m. Take a path on the left, signed 'walk 5', which goes downhill and along the lower edge of the wood through drifts of broom, laden with flowers in June. Go over two stiles to a track junction at the end of the wood. Cross and take the left track continuing along the bottom of the valley, past Westertown Farm.

2 Cross the small footbridge beside a ford and wind up the far side, between gorse, and into a short stretch of forest. Cross the burn again on a plank bridge and climb the far side to a fenced track leading up the hillside. Curlews and lapwings call and display in spring and early summer in the pastures on either side. Higher up the path runs along a terrace below a forest, where you may find chickweed wintergreen and petty whin. Go through a gate and continue below the forest, then the path turns in amongst the trees.

3 At the 3-armed signpost turn right onto the Speyside Way (signed for Ballindalloch) and climb gently through the trees. Then the path winds right and begins to descend. Leave the forest by a gate and follow the signed long track left, along the edge of the trees to the end of the wood. Climb the clear quartzite path to the top of Carn Daimh, where you might hear golden plovers. Pause here to enjoy the superb view from the summit, south to Ben Avon and Beinn a'Bhuird and the other Cairngorms, and north-east to Ben Rinnes and Corriehabbie Hill.

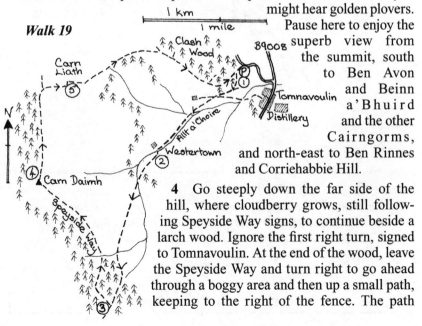

Walk 19

4 Go steeply down the far side of the hill, where cloudberry grows, still following Speyside Way signs, to continue beside a larch wood. Ignore the first right turn, signed to Tomnavoulin. At the end of the wood, leave the Speyside Way and turn right to go ahead through a boggy area and then up a small path, keeping to the right of the fence. The path becomes clearer as it gets higher and crosses the broad shoulder of Carn Liath.

5 Descend steadily towards the valley, cross the fence at a stile and slant across the hillside down towards the near corner of a wood. The path runs along above the trees, winds round a corner and across the field to a gate into Clash Wood. Beyond, turn right and descend the pleasant track with lovely views across the valley. Turn into the wood and down to the car park.

Petty Whin

Practicals

Type of walk: A challenging airy walk. Well signposted. Remember to wear suitable footwear and carry waterproofs as the Highland weather can change quickly and dramatically.

Total distance:	6½ miles/10.5km
Time:	4 hours
Maps:	OS Explorer 419/Landranger 36

20

Drumin Castle and Bridgend of Glenlivet

Park in the car park at the Glenlivet Distillery, where the Smugglers' Trails start, grid ref 195289. Access this along the B9008 from the north, or the B9136 from the south, to Bridge of Livet, then take the minor road up Glenlivet to the distillery. It is well signed.

Whisky taxes imposed by the British Government in the second half of the 18th century and well into the 19th, led to illicit distilling. Glenlivet, wild and remote, with just the right climate and terrain for making whisky, once had over 200 illicit stills. Smugglers moved their whisky out of the glen along secret paths, often difficult to use in inclement weather.

Glenlivet Packhorse Bridge

The **George Smith Smugglers trail** follows the River Livet to Drumin Castle. George Smith had the first licensed distillery in Glenlivet and his house is passed at the start of the walk. He worked hard to develop his distillery, battling against the climate and the terrain and also the unreformed smugglers who continually undermined his work.

1 Return to the road and turn left following the Speyside Way and Smugglers' Trail signs. Go on past Minmore House Hotel, once the home of George Smith, founder of the distillery. Turn left onto a path, at the end of the policies, which is fenced and follows the edge of the field through two gates. Turn right to go along the top of a wood, full of chickweed wintergreen and bilberry. At the end ignore the signed right branch (your return route), turn left and walk along the edge of the wood, with fields below and wooded slopes above. At the road turn right and then in 22yds/20m, left, up a small path into more woodland. Join a track and walk right until you reach a barrier onto a road again. Turn left and walk the verge until you are past the Glenlivet Community Surgery, then take the right turn signed to Drumin Castle.

2 At the foot of the hill pass through a car park to take a small gate which gives access to the castle, a fortified towerhouse, built in the 14th century and once the stronghold of Alexander Stewart, Earl of Buchan, who was known as the 'Wolf of Badenoch'. Follow the path round the base of the spur, between the Livet and Avon rivers, on which the castle is built and from where there are lovely views. Continue up a hairpin bend, and at the top enjoy more fine views. Then turn right into the walled garden for yet another splendid view of the ruined castle. Return to the path and walk on round the side to visit the ruins, which have been stabilised. Then go back and down steps to return to the car park.

River Avon

Drumin Castle

B9008

R. Livet

Bridge of Livet

Bridgend of Livet

Sch

B9136

½ km

½ mile

N

Minmore House

Walk 20

The Glenlivet Distillery

3 Turn left on the road and cross the road bridge over the Livet. Descend steps on the right to walk along the riverside, enjoying the pools and rapids, the herons and dippers, and possibly roe deer. Wood cranesbill and sweet cicely grow in profusion on the banks. Then cross the lovely waterway by a wooden footbridge and continue on along another stretch of the river to reach the B-road.

4 Turn left to cross the river by the Bridge of Livet. Walk on with care along the road verge through the village of Bridgend of Glenlivet. Turn right into another car park and down steps to a viewpoint overlooking a dramatic old packhorse bridge. Then return through the village and past the cemetery to re-cross the Livet Bridge and climb the path to the road by the school. Step, right, into a fenced way beside the road, then along the top of a field to rejoin your outward path at the edge of the wood. Turn left and return to the distillery visitor centre, where you may wish to enjoy the café.

Heron

Wood Cranesbill

Practicals

Type of walk: A delightful walk along grassy paths, woodland tracks and surfaced trails.

Complete distance:	3½ miles/5.5km
Time:	2–3 hours
Maps:	OS Explorer 419/Landranger 36

21

Ben Rinnes

Park in the small car park at the start of the path, grid ref 284359. If full there is a space in a small quarry a short distance up the road, and a lot of space on the verge. Please do not obstruct the gate leading onto the hill. To access this take the B9009 south out of Dufftown and after 3miles/5 km turn right onto a minor road signed to Milltown of Edinvillie. The car park is on the left ¼ mile/0.5km along this road.

Ben Rinnes is a very popular hill, near several centres of population and easy of access. It is a Corbett, 2730ft/840m high, and is the second highest hill in Banffshire. It has suffered badly from erosion but the Friends of Ben Rinnes have raised money to have the path repaired; it is now excellent.

Like the Cairngorms Ben Rinnes is a **granite hill** and has several tors on its summit, where the outcropping granite has weathered into horizontal blocks. This layering is called sheet jointing and is particularly spectacular on Lady's Chair. These tors on Ben Rinnes are called Scurrans, from the Gaelic for a little tor, Sgoran.

Lady's Chair, Ben Rinnes

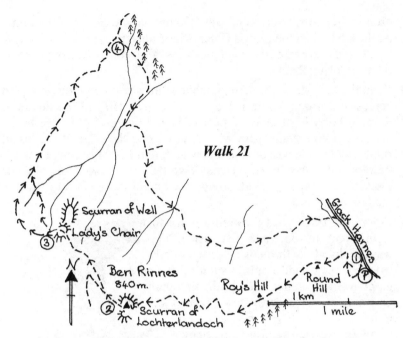

Walk 21

1 Beyond the gate, follow the well-made path as it traverses the hillside. Continue up the steep nose at the end of the ridge in easy zigzags and then the gradient eases at the top of the first hill, called Round Hill. Go through a stile by a gate and continue up the relatively gentle slope to the top of Roy's Hill. Red grouse scatter noisily as you climb. Descend slightly and then climb to the Scurran of Lochterlandoch on the zigzagging path with steps in the steepest places. High up the granite tors of the Scurran come into view. Carry on to the base of the tors and wind round to the right to climb easily up to the trig point on the highest one. The view from here is magnificent, over Speyside and the 'Whisky Glens', and out over the Moray Firth to the hills of Ross and Sutherland.

2 If the weather is deteriorating, or during the shooting season, return by the ascent route. To continue on this circular route walk to the right away from the summit tor following a wide track through the heather along the top of the hill. Where it begins to swing left take a less obvious track forking right, which soon becomes a path heading for another

Cloudberry

group of tors, the Scurran of Well. Go up into the centre of the group on the left, called the Lady's Chair, where amazing granite rocks have weathered into heaps like piled pancakes. You will wish to spend some time exploring them.

3 From the far side of this group, make your way on an indistinct path across to a broad gentle ridge, called Baby's Hill, in the distance. Remain fairly high to avoid peat hags and two gullies where burns descend. Join a small path which runs along the crest of the broad ridge. Look for leaves of cloudberry and, in the right season, its white flowers and amber berries. Head down the ridge towards an obvious track, which starts in a wide stony area. Follow its bendy way down to the foot of the hill.

4 Before the track goes through a fence turn right along an old track just inside. The way climbs a little through a pleasant lightly wooded area beside a burn, then fords the burn on convenient stones and climbs gradually up onto the often damp lower slopes of Ben Rinnes from where there are good retrospective views towards the Spey Valley. Eventually the track comes downhill, crosses a burn and ends at a gate onto the road. Turn right and walk back through the steep sided Glack Harnes, downhill all the way, to your car.

Red Grouse

Practicals

Type of walk: A straightforward climb up a good path, giving splendid views. The return route described is pathless in places so needs some navigational ability and is best not attempted in mist or bad weather. Grouse shooting takes place on the estate so from August 12th remember to return by your route of ascent.

Complete distance:	8 miles/13km or 5 miles/8km
Time:	5 hours or 3 hours
Maps:	OS Explorer 424/Landranger 28

22

Glen Fiddich and the Gownie Path

Park in the small car park beside the Telford bridge at Craigellachie, grid ref 286451. To access this from the south, turn left off the A95 just beyond the sign for Keith and Craigellachie (also A95) but before you reach the actual junction. Drive down to the parking and picnic area.

Craigellachie Bridge, built in 1814, was designed by Thomas Telford. It was the first bridge crossing of the Spey. Until then the only way to cross was by ferry, which was fine in good conditions but dangerous in wild weather when the river was in spate. The bridge has a high single arch span to allow floodwaters plenty of room to pass beneath it. This would not have been possible with a masonry bridge so Telford used cast iron, the first cast iron bridge in Scotland.

Dufftown, home to seven distilleries, is known as the whisky capital of Scotland. This walk goes past three of them, the best known of which is Glenfiddich.

Glenfiddich distillery

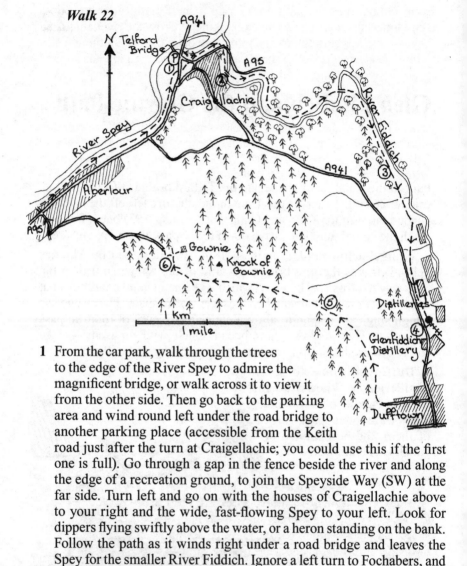

Walk 22

N Telford Bridge

A941

A95

Craigellachie

River Spey

Aberlour

A95

River Fiddich

A941

③

Gownie

Knock of
Gownie

⑥

⑤

Distilleries

1 Km

1 mile

Glenfiddich
Distillery

④

Dufftown

1 From the car park, walk through the trees
to the edge of the River Spey to admire the
magnificent bridge, or walk across it to view it
from the other side. Then go back to the parking
area and wind round left under the road bridge to
another parking place (accessible from the Keith
road just after the turn at Craigellachie; you could use this if the first
one is full). Go through a gap in the fence beside the river and along
the edge of a recreation ground, to join the Speyside Way (SW) at the
far side. Turn left and go on with the houses of Craigellachie above
to your right and the wide, fast-flowing Spey to your left. Look for
dippers flying swiftly above the water, or a heron standing on the bank.
Follow the path as it winds right under a road bridge and leaves the
Spey for the smaller River Fiddich. Ignore a left turn to Fochabers, and
go ahead for Dufftown. Walk on beside a car park and a camping area
surrounded by lovely open woodland.

2 Go on to cross the bridge over the River Fiddich and then through
a barrier where a notice warns you of landslips ahead, repaired for
walkers only. The way is delightful, through mature deciduous woodland down in the deeply incised valley, with the river foaming to your

74

right. Sometimes the path goes along a shelf or through a cutting, sometimes it is raised up on an embankment. Cross the river again and beyond another cutting emerge into more open country, although still with woods to your right. The repair work where the path has slipped is perfectly adequate and there is no difficulty in crossing it.

3 Continue, now high above the river. Through birch you can see the first distillery warehouses below on the left. Ignore a footpath to the left signed Isla Way, and walk ahead past a derelict distillery (Convalmore, which was closed in 1986, although Grants still use the warehouses). Cross a road leading to the Balvenie Distillery and continue beside railway lines with carriages, to the platform of the Keith and Dufftown Light Railway. Walk along the platform and turn right at the end of the station buildings as indicated by a signpost. Go out to the main road and turn left to walk the pavement.

4 The road runs past the Glenfiddich Distillery which has a visitor centre and an excellent café where you might like to pause. Return to the main road and walk on into Dufftown. As you round a bend the clocktower in the centre comes into view. Look for Hill Street on the right, and walk along it past the football ground and out into fields. Cross a burn on a bridge and continue uphill as directed by a Scottish Rights of Way Society (SRWS) sign to Aberlour; this is the Gownie path. Follow it, right, along the hillside below a wood. Enjoy the wide views out over Dufftown and Glen Fiddich. At the end of the woodland, go ahead on a waymarked fenced grassy path, which runs between fields and then down over a burn. Cross a track and turn left beyond it to climb a pleasant grassy swathe between newly planted trees, on the edge of a conifer wood. Watch out for flocks of siskins feeding on cones.

5 At the top corner cross into heathland and cut across to a belt of larch, beyond which the path leads into open heather, with scattered pines and birch. Turn left by a fence and follow the path between embankments covered with gorse. Go over the summit of the ridge and down to a forestry plantation. Press on down the track, which is grassy at first, later becoming sandy and then reinforced. There are fields on the left and a fine view of Ben Rinnes.

Broom

75

6 At a cross of tracks, turn left and go downhill to a corner where the track becomes metalled. Carry on downhill, quite steeply, into Aberlour. Cross the main road and go down the left side of the square, signed to the Alice Littler Park and the SW. Turn right on the old station platform and continue on the track until it meets up with the SW. Beyond an industrial estate stride the path as it continues into mature beech woodland with the Spey away to the left. The bank becomes steeper and the path runs in a cutting and then a short tunnel. The bridge at Craigellachie appears in the distance. Follow the path under the A95, go past the Craigellachie Hotel (where a sign welcomes walkers) and under another road bridge. Turn left to walk back along the edge of the recreation ground and under the bridge by the Spey to return to your car.

Siskin

Practicals

Type of walk: Pleasing. Mainly along disused railway lines, which give very easy walking. The Gownie path over the hill is well way-marked by the SRWS and although it climbs to about 1,000ft you start quite high. There are two sections of road walking which are unavoidable, both about 1 mile long.

Complete distance:	12 miles/19km
Time:	5–6 hours.
Maps:	OS Explorer 424/Landranger 28

23

Randolph's Leap

Park in the large car park at Logie Steading grid ref 007505, where there is an excellent café, farm shop, and several craft shops. To reach this, take the A940 from Grantown to Forres. Turn west onto the B9007 and in a short distance turn right into the entrance to Logie Steading and continue to the car park.

Randolph's Leap is named after Thomas Randolph, Earl of Moray, who lived at Darnaway on the far side of the gorge. In fact he did not leap it. It was Alastair Cumming, eldest son of Sir Alexander Cumming, who did this. The Cummings had been Rangers of Darnaway Forest but fell out of favour with Randolph and his uncle, King Robert the Bruce, and they were dismissed. Alastair took 1,000 men to attack Randolph, but they were ambushed and driven back to the river, where he and three of his men leaped across.

The **two flood stones** mark the level, 50ft/15m above normal, to which the River Findhorn and its

Randolph's Leap

tributaries rose in August 1829, after three days of
torrential rain in the Monadhliath. The whole
lower valley was flooded and devastated.

1 Go through the children's play area and along
the wide grassy path round a field. Turn right
down a steep path towards the River Findhorn
and out onto a little promontory giving fine
views in both directions. Wind round its side
and down through beech trees on a good
path towards a lower level. The path
runs above the
spectacular
river to its

Walk 23

confluence with
the River Divie,
where both rivers snake
their way through rocky
channels with waterfalls. Here
the path winds left to follow the
Divie, also in a gorge, until it comes
out onto the B9007 just beside a bridge.
Cross the bridge and walk up the road for
220yds/200m to a small gate on the right, where
there is an information board. Go through and down steps to take the
right-hand, lower path, which winds round a cliff above the Divie and
brings you down through fine woodland to the confluence with the
Findhorn again. Here is a stone that marks the flood level of 1829.

2 Walk left along the Findhorn, still on a good path through beech and
pine, and enjoy the river scenery. A fence on the right closes off a path
which has fallen away; so go left up a shallow valley, then back right
to rejoin the original path. (If you go right here you can get down to
the river's edge, but no further). The main path carries on left, round
a corner to the narrow chasm of Randolph's Leap. Go down steps to a
viewing platform. There is a ladder to the river. People jump in, swim
through the channel and climb back up the ladder.

3 Follow the path round to a junction where another flood stone is set
back a little. The widest path goes left, back up to the road, and if you
wish to end your walk here this is the way to go. This walk takes the
right turn to continue along by the Findhorn. At a path junction take
the left turn, which climbs steeply, crosses a wooden bridge and then
gradually goes down again. This is an old estate path running through

lovely mature woodland with occasional huge trees. Ignore all side paths and continue on the main one as it takes you up and over the many cliffs and, from it, gives you fine river views through the trees. You may see dippers and grey wagtails, and occasionally salmon leap. There are a few wet patches, and towards the end there is a place where at some time a landslip has occurred. Step up a metre or so on stones to a higher level and follow the narrow path round, with care; it is quite stable but somewhat exposed. Then it comes downhill again and eventually out to a minor road by a high stone bridge.

4 Turn left at the road and walk uphill away from the river, round hairpin bends. Where the road comes out of the trees and there is a field on the left, look for an entry at the edge of the wood. Walk on along a ride following a faint path through the grass along the edge of the field until the fence turns right to go steeply uphill. About 11yds/10m to the left is the start of a forest track. Contour through the forest, below an area of clearfell, and finally join the road about ¼ mile/0.5 km from Randolph's Leap. Walk on down to the bridge over the Divie and take the path on the left to retrace your steps along the riverbank to Logie Steading.

Grey Wagtail

Practicals

Type of walk: This is a spectacular walk with some superb river scenery. There are unprotected cliffs so children should be closely supervised and dogs kept on leads; the area is also subject to flash floods so be aware of the weather in the hills. The Findhorn, like the Spey, drains a large mountainous catchment.

Complete distance: 4 miles/6.5km.

Time: 2–3 hours

Maps: OS Explorer 419 and 422/Landranger 27

24

Monaughty Wood
and Pluscarden Abbey

Park in the Forestry car park for Torrieston Walks, grid ref 164589. To access this take the B9010 south from Elgin and turn right for Miltonduff, Torrieston Forest Walks and Pluscarden.

Pluscarden Priory was founded in 1230. At the time of the Reformation it fell into disuse. Four hundred years later it was given to the Benedictine community of Prinknash by Lord Colum Crichton-Stuart. The community took up residence in 1948 and work on the building continues today. In 1947 it was elevated to an Abbey. It is open all year and admission is free.

Pluscarden Abbey

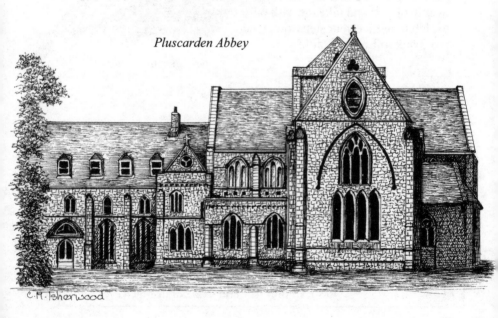

C.M. Sherwood

Heldon Hill, behind the Abbey, would have been covered with deciduous woodland originally, but the trees were reduced by cutting, burning and grazing. By the early 19th.century it was covered only in heather. Then James, the 5th Earl of Fife, planted the whole area with larch, Scots pine and beech, raising the seedlings in the grounds of the then ruined Pluscarden Priory. The woodland was acquired by the Forestry Commission in the 1920s and further planting took place, notably of Douglas fir.

1 Walk across the grass past the toilets and up steps to join a path along a bank. Turn left, then after 110yds/100m take a right turn, which leads up more steps and along a winding path through magnificent tall

Monaughty Wood

Torrieston

Walk 24

Heldon Hill

Milton

½ Km

½ mile

Pluscarden Abbey

conifers. Climb gently to reach a wider path. Go left and soon begin to contour, listening for coal tits searching for insects. Ignore the waymarked path on the right and carry on, now gently downhill, past an area of clearfell to come to a forest track.

2 Turn right and climb slightly. Follow the track along a terrace through the woodland, with occasional glimpses to the left out over the wide fertile valley below. At the Y-junction take the left (lower) track, and after 110yds/100m, just before a small cleared area, look for a path going back at an angle and quite steeply downhill between beech trees. It soon becomes less steep and slants down the edge of the forest with views of Pluscarden Abbey and its fine vegetable garden to the right. Continue on through mature beech along the walled path.

3 At the bottom of the slope turn right and cross a stile following a sign for 'Abbey'. Walk round the edge of a field to a gate in the precinct wall, which gives access to the Abbey grounds. Then return round the field to the stile, cross and continue straight ahead, signed 'Elgin'. Follow this lovely walled path along the lower edge of the forest. The path comes out into the access track for Mill Cottage and then on to the road.

4 Walk straight ahead following the sign for Elgin. Go past a house on the right, then before the next house there is a wide forestry turning space and track. Here join the waymarked path running along the forest edge, lined with rowan and wild cherry trees, which brings you back to the car park. Here wrens chide from the bushes and goldcrests and coal tits are busy in the Douglas and silver fir trees which tower above.

Wild Cherry

Practicals

Type of walk: Idyllically peaceful especially if the Abbey bells are ringing in the distance and the wood pigeons are cooing quietly. Good paths and tracks.

Complete distance:	4 miles/6.5km
Time:	3 hours
Maps:	OS Explorer 423/Landranger 28

25

The Wood of Ordiequish

Park either in the car park for Slorach's Wood, grid ref 341562, reached by turning left and driving the very rough forest track, or drive 55yds/50m further along the road and park, on the right, in the Earth Pillars car park, grid ref 336564. If you choose the latter you will have to walk up the forest track for ¼ mile/0.5 km to the Slorach's Wood car park. To reach both these car parks take the minor road signed to the Police Station in Fochabers and continue along it for two miles.

Ordiequish Wood, in Moray, is a mixed conifer woodland on the banks of Ordiequish Burn. It has a maze of old paths and tracks that date back to the 19th century.

The Jean Carr Stone is reached about a third of the way round the walk. The stone is reputed to be her final resting place. She was a very disturbed character, after being kept in her room by her father until he died when she took refuge in the woods. Later she had a child that was taken from her by the authorities and it eventually died. Then

Jean Carr's Stone

she thought the only way to have children was to take other peoples. She was found dead lying close to her stone with a baby blanket in her hand.

Ordiequish has cycling routes of varying difficulty. For example, the soup dragon is easy, the Gordzilla is moderate together with the Haggis. The Gully Monster, seen from above on this walk, is an awesome trail of monster proportions.

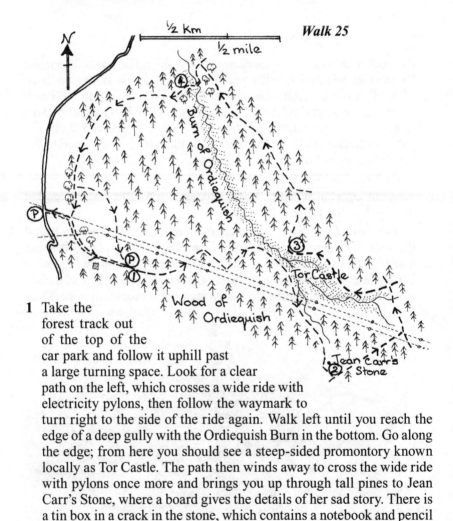

Walk 25

1 Take the forest track out of the top of the car park and follow it uphill past a large turning space. Look for a clear path on the left, which crosses a wide ride with electricity pylons, then follow the waymark to turn right to the side of the ride again. Walk left until you reach the edge of a deep gully with the Ordiequish Burn in the bottom. Go along the edge; from here you should see a steep-sided promontory known locally as Tor Castle. The path then winds away to cross the wide ride with pylons once more and brings you up through tall pines to Jean Carr's Stone, where a board gives the details of her sad story. There is a tin box in a crack in the stone, which contains a notebook and pencil for the use of visitors.

2 Go on left up the path to a forest track and turn left. Be aware that you share this part of the route with mountain bikers. Cross the burn and the pylon ride again and turn left at a track junction. The mountain bike trail, called Gully Monster, goes off on the left and shortly after this the walkers' path also branches off to the left (the waymark is some distance along the path). This small path winds down along the edge of the spectacular gully of the Ordiequish Burn. The views from this side are much more dramatic than those on the way up. But the most alarming view of all is the sight of the mountain bike trail, a narrow way winding along the side of the gully some 20ft/6m below you with blind sharp corners, narrow ledges and a long drop below it.

Wren

3 Eventually the path leaves the edge of the ravine and heads across the hillside, where it joins a track and bends left. Look for red squirrels, and cones which they have eaten, and you may see roe deer. Wrens scold from the undergrowth. At a waymark walk on straight-ahead, until at the lower edge of the wood you reach a T-junction. Turn left here and descend through lovely woodland to the burn. Cross the bridge then climb the very steep steps on the far side; there is a seat at the top, which may be welcome.

4 Wind on through dark forest of western hemlock, then out into an area of clearfell where native trees are regenerating. There is a fine wide view over the Spey Valley and out to the sea. Go back into pine wood and contour along the lower edge, ignoring a track going right, until you reach a waymark directing you left, uphill, on a small path. (If you left your car in the lower car park carry straight on here to the track, then turn right and walk back down to the road where you go left.) Soon the uphill path levels out and runs along behind gorse bushes until it comes downhill to the car park.

Practicals

Type of walk: Good paths, well-waymarked. Straightforward. One steep climb up steps.

Complete distance:	4½ miles/7.4km
Time:	3 hours
Maps:	OS Explorer 424/Landranger 28

26

Dunnyduff Wood and
the Falls of Tarnash, Keith

Park in Reidhaven Square off the A96 at the south end of Keith, grid ref 432502.

The **Falls of Tarnash**, near Keith, have always been a favourite with local people. There is a lovely cast-iron bridge above the plummetting water.

The **Great Spotted Woodpecker** is an inhabitant of woodlands and parks, depending for food and nesting sites on old timber. It advertises its presence by a mechanical call, a loud vibrating rattle, produced by rapid repeated blows of its strong bill upon a trunk or branch and sometimes a telegraph pole, even a metal one. The nesting hole is bored horizontally for a few inches, in soft or decaying wood, then it continues downwards for about six inches or more. Five to seven white eggs are laid at the foot of this perpendicular boring on wood chips, generally during the second half of May.

Great Spotted Woodpecker

1 Walk out of the square, cross the main road (A96) and continue straight ahead down the minor road until it runs out into the countryside. At a sign for the Falls of Tarnash, ignore the green track that goes straight

ahead. Here this walk turns left, continuing on the road. Go downhill, right, to cross the Burn of Drum and immediately bear left onto a path through bushes and scrub with the burn to your left; this used to be part of Keith's golf course but was dug up in the 'Dig for Victory' campaign in the 1939–45 war. The path goes gently uphill and then rejoins the road.

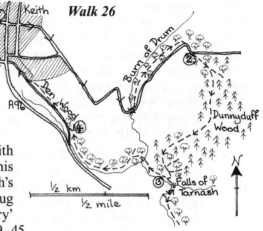

2 Cross and walk up a forestry track opposite, into Dunnyduff Wood. About 110yds/100m further on, turn right at a sign to climb steps onto a delightful path running through hazel and birch, then coming out into

Falls of Tarnash

high pine woodland where you may see a great spotted woodpecker. There is a viewpoint on the right looking out over Keith. Cross another path in an area of clearfell and carry on into more pine wood, this time with young beech understorey. Go across the end of a forest track and where the path divides take the right branch, heading downhill. Soon it begins to wind round in large zigzags and you can hear the waterfall. At the signpost, turn left and go upstream; first admire the falls with the fine cast iron bridge above them, then cross the bridge and go on to the bigger fall on the next burn.

3 Return to the signpost and walk ahead with the burn on your left. Look out for grey wagtails and maybe a dipper. The path emerges from the trees into the open, then crosses the burn on a sturdy bridge and climbs steeply up the bank on the far side. At a T-junction, turn left and go gently down again. Now the way is a wide path which rises and then contours through a steep narrow beech wood, Den Wood, at first above the A96, then above a minor road.

4 Take the right fork at the Y-junction, then the left fork at the next one, so that you keep more or less on the level. Eventually you reach bungalows and the path comes down onto a road. Walk along it for a short way and then wind left and uphill until you reach the main road again. Cross with care and go ahead, following signs for Keith Square. Turn right along Mid Street, lined with solid grey stone cottages, which will bring you back to Reidhaven Square and your car.

Practicals

Type of walk: Easy, good paths, well-signed. Some unavoidable minor road walking

Total Distance:	4 miles/6.5km
Time:	2–3 hours
Maps:	OS Explorer 424/Landranger 28

27

Huntly and the River Deveron

Park in the free car park just north of the Square, grid ref 530401.

The site of **Huntly** is believed to have been settled since before the 12th century. It was much expanded by the Duke of Gordon on a gridiron street pattern in the 1770s and, because there has been little

Huntly Castle

further large scale development of the town, it has retained most of its traditional character, street pattern and historic buildings.

Passed early on this walk is a small green mound, the motte, once the site of the **first castle** at Huntly. The earthworks were created from a low natural mound overlooking the point where the rivers Bogie and Deveron meet; this was an important crossing place. At the time this early castle was inhabited it would have been ringed with a defensive timber palisade.

On a visit to the castle (recommended) notice the mainly intact great inscription on the south front. It says **'GEORGE GORDVN FIRST MARQVIS OF HUVNTLIE 16 HENRIETTE STEWART MARQVESSE OF HUNTLIE O2**. This proclaimed the rise of the Gordons from earls to marquises.

Walk 27

1 Return to the road and turn right towards the castle. Cross a road by the war memorial and walk ahead down a double avenue of lime trees, gifted to the nation in 1925 by Sir Leybourne Davidson of Huntly Lodge, to reach the castle which you may wish to visit. Go left round the base of the mound, the original

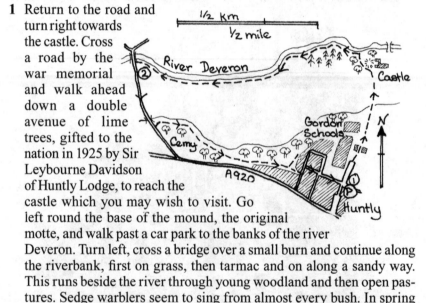

motte, and walk past a car park to the banks of the river Deveron. Turn left, cross a bridge over a small burn and continue along the riverbank, first on grass, then tarmac and on along a sandy way. This runs beside the river through young woodland and then open pastures. Sedge warblers seem to sing from almost every bush. In spring milkmaids and sweet cicely carpet the bank, with kingcups down by the water. Keep along the riverbank, ignoring paths off to the left.

2 At a road bridge over the river, go up steps, turn left to walk the pavement. Soon the road comes to the outskirts of the town. Just before the cemetery go left along a good path, which runs outside the cemetery wall, leading into beech woodland, carpeted in spring with wood anemone, celandine and white allium. The path leads to a mown area

under trees and a seat. Walk ahead, cross a road and pick up the path again on the far side, leading through more woodland. Go straight ahead at a fork to join a track, which leads out to a road. Turn left, then right onto West Park road. Carry on to the war memorial and turn right to return to the car park.

Wood anemones
and celandines

Practicals

Type of walk: Short and level through very pleasant countryside

Complete distance:	2 miles/3.5km
Time:	2 hours if you include a visit to the castle
Maps:	OS Explorer 425/Landranger 29

28

Knock Hill

Park near the right-angled bend after the farm at grid ref 547553. To access this, take the A95 Keith to Banff road until the B9022, from Huntly, comes in on your right, just before the Glenbarry Hotel. Continue on the A-road for approximately ½ mile/1km. Immediately beyond a cottage on the left and before a bend, turn left onto an unobtrusive, unsigned, metalled lane. Drive the narrow way, through Swilebog farm and go on to a T-junction. There is parking for about 5 cars on the left.

Knock Hill (1465ft/450m) is visible for miles around and the view from the summit is a superb 360 degrees. You can see the whole of the Moray Plain to Bennachie and then, behind Ben Rinnes, more hills and mountains. The Bin of Cullen is most obvious. The land below is a glorious patchwork of gorse, woodland and arable fields.

The sedge-warbler, a summer migrant, arrives late in April. It haunts dense bushes and

On top of Knock Hill

other low-growing vegetation, usually close to a ditch, stream, small pond or a marsh. It advertises its presence with an erratic, often harsh frequent chattering but is rarely seen.

Sedge Warbler

1 Turn right out of the parking area and walk a few steps along the surfaced lane to take a gate gap/kissing gate on the left. The distinct path goes up through a grassy clearing, edged with gorse, in birch woodland. Soon the trees close in on the path. In spring, look for wood anemones and violets in profusion below the trees. Listen for sedge warblers, willow warblers and chiffchaffs as you go. The path emerges onto heather with scattered gorse and birch.

2 Go through a kissing gate and continue straight up the hillside, through more heather and scattered young trees. The eroded path could be quite slippery after rain as it is very steep. In places it has become a deep groove in the peat and here walkers are making alternative paths at the edges. The underlying rock is quartzite.

3 Continue on over three ridges, where the angle eases and then the way steepens once more. Here you might spot wheatears and red grouse. Near the summit the path levels. Pass through a kissing gate in a new fence and walk on to the trig point. Pause at both cairns; one marks the

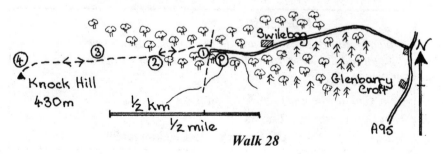

Swilebog

Knock Hill
430m

½ km

½ mile

Glenbarry
Croft

A95

Walk 28

summit and the other is a memorial to Martin James Gilles, instigator of the Stone Run.

4 Return, with care, by the same steep route as there is no other way off.

Wheatear

CMI

Practicals

Type of walk: Both ascent and descent of the hill are steep and difficult but the views from the top make it a very worthwhile challenge.

Complete distance:	1½ miles/2.5km
Time:	2 hours
Maps:	OS Explorer 425/Landranger 29

29

Gight Woods

Park in the Forestry Commission's Braes of Gight car park, grid ref 833399. Access this from the B9005 Methlick to Fyvie road, about 3 miles/5km out of Methlick.

The now ruinous **Gight Castle** was built around 1560. It stands on a steep wooded hill above the gorge of the River Ythan and all around is quiet peaceful parkland. The Gordon lairds, who owned the castle, were not so peaceful. Most died violently until Catherine Gordon, the 13th laird, wed Jack Byron, who gambled away the estate. Catherine and Jack were the parents of the poet Lord Byron.

Live birds would have been housed in the **Doocot**, or dovecot, throughout the winter. These would have provided fresh meat for 'the big house' during the winter when meat was short or non-existent. The inside of the building would have been criss-crossed with many perches.

Doocot, Gight Woods

Walk 29

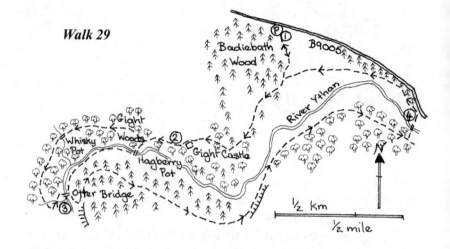

1 Leave the car park and walk the forestry track through Badiebath Wood, past a quarry and over a burn. Carry on uphill on a good track through clearfell. At the top, the way becomes grassy and moves into mature deciduous trees, passing between stone gate posts and on through a kissing gate. Cross the pasture beyond, keep right of the ruin of Gight Gastle (which is unsafe) to go through another kissing gate into the Scottish Wildlife Trust's Gight Woods Reserve.

2 Follow the strimmed path downhill to a path junction and take the right branch steeply uphill. Go past the ruins of an old Doocot, then the remains of a bothy with a fine chimney, and on into mature woodland with many splendid beech trees. The path follows the top wall of the reserve, then descends a short distance to cross a bridge at Whisky Pot. Go up steps at the far side into an open area with broom and some young trees. Beside a stand of larch the path starts to wind downhill, with steps in places, through hazel. Cross a small burn on a bridge, then continue down in zigzags. Look for bugle and stitchwort beside the path.

3 Cross Otter Bridge over the River Ythan. Turn right on a small path, which in a few metres, leads round a stand of conifers to join a grassy forest track. Turn left onto the track and continue to a gate out of the forest; a sign here asks you to be careful near cows and to keep all dogs on leads, and another sign says 'Methlick 3 miles'. Carry on along the track, going through small gates beside farm gates and then coming out into open country. There are steep slopes and trees to the right and river flats to the left, where swallows and martins swoop over the water

and you may hear the continuous churring of a grasshopper warbler. Press on into another wooded area and then take a track, on the left, which crosses the Ythan again on a substantial bridge and takes you out to the road.

4 Turn left immediately onto a reinforced track which soon becomes grassy, and runs along below a wood. Cross a track then go on between fences, through fields, and into Badiebath Wood again through stone gate posts. At the forest track turn right and walk uphill to your car.

Grasshopper Warbler

Practicals

Type of walk: A very pleasing ramble.

Complete distance:	4½ miles/7.4km
Time:	2–3 hours
Maps:	OS Explorer 426/Landranger 30

30

Aden Country Park
and Deer Abbey

Park in the main car park of Aden Country Park, grid ref 982479. Access is along the A950, 1¼ miles/2km, west of Mintlaw.

Before it became Aden Country Park, the estate was owned for almost 200 years by the **Russells of Aden,** pronounced as **Ah-den**. They transformed it from a bare landscape into extensive woodland and shrubs. They sold the estate in 1937 and for the next 40 years it became considerably neglected. In 1975 the District Council set about restoring the heart of the estate, 230 acres of parkland, and it is now managed by Aberdeenshire Council.

Old Deer is set in the wooded valley of South Ugie Water, near the ruins of a **Cistercian abbey**, founded in 1218. The 9th century

Deer Abbey

Latin manuscript, the ***Book of Deer,*** belonged to the monks of a nearby monastery (location now no longer known). In the margins of the book are notes about the book written in the 11th-12th century, the earliest known examples of written Scots Gaelic.

In the early 18th century the Episcopalian villagers of **Old Deer** threw out the Presbyterian minister, the incident known as the 'Rabbling of Deer'. Today both denominations are happily established. The parish church stands at the end of the main street and the Episcopalian church opposite.

1 Walk from the car park to the Agricultural Heritage Centre, where you may like to visit the restaurant or the Centre itself, both located in fine buildings. Stroll back towards the car park and, on your way, take a footpath, on the right signed to Hareshowe. Go past the Nursery and turn onto a path on the left and bear left at its end. Head on with fields to your right and car parking to your left. At its end go along the entrance road and, in 55yds/50m, turn right on a good surfaced path, which leads through birch and beech woodland. Just before the main path reaches a road, turn right on a smaller path, then take the next left turn.

2 At a T-junction, with fields ahead, turn left again and wind through young woodland, ignoring left and right turns, until the path joins a wide bridlepath by a line of spruce trees. Turn right, cross a tiny cattle creep and turn left along the edge of the wood with the burn, Ugie Water, below on the right. Cross the burn on a footbridge and walk ahead with the arboretum to your right. Just before another rather

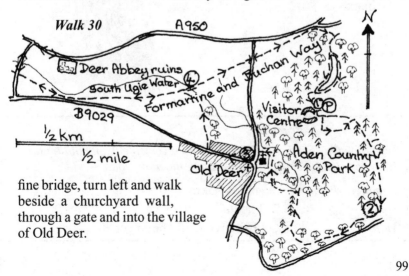

fine bridge, turn left and walk beside a churchyard wall, through a gate and into the village of Old Deer.

3 Cross the road (B9030) and walk ahead up the wide main street. At the end of the houses, on the right, follow signs for the Formartine and Buchan Way, along a field margin under stately beeches and up to join the old railway line. Carry on, left, along the pleasant track, which is edged with birch, through the valley of the South Ugie Water. The river is often visible and if you are lucky you may see an osprey. Where the track crosses a road, turn right, cross the narrow bridge over the river and turn right again at the main road (A950). Head on with care along the verge for 220yds/200m to the ruins of Deer Abbey, enclosed by a high wall with fruit trees trained against it. You will enjoy exploring the ruins. Then return along the roads to the old railway track and retrace your steps.

4 Ignore the path where you joined the track and continue along the way until it reaches the main road. Do not cross, but take a path leading right into delightful woodland, full of willow warblers, wrens and chaffinches and where you may see a treecreeper. In a very short distance, turn right on another path and then almost immediately left. This brings you to the lake in Aden Country Park and you can stroll down either side. Bear right and then, immediately left at the end, to walk round the left side of the main building to return to the car park.

Treecreeper

Practicals

Type of walk: *Level, good paths through very pleasant countryside. Take care on the short distance along the main road.*

Complete distance:	3½ miles/5.5km
Time:	2–3 hours
Maps:	OS Explorer 427/Landranger 30

31

Cruden Bay to Bullers of Buchan

Park at Cruden Bay, grid ref 093362. Turn off the A975 onto the minor road to the harbour. The main parking area lies on the same side of the road as the church and if facing the church it is on the right.

The Village above **Bullers of Buchan**, the name given to the cove below the settlement, was a small cliff top fishing community that owed its existence to the cove where fishermen could beach their boats. All their gear and catch had to be manhandled up the steep cliffs from the shore. This really brought about the demise of the village as a fishing station.

The Pot, Bullers of Buchan

Slains Castle was erected in 1597 by the 9th Earl of Errol. It has been rebuilt and added to over the centuries. The 20th Earl sold the castle in 1916 and it fell into disrepair and is today a dramatic clifftop ruin.

1 Walk out of the end of the car park on a wide track through woodland. At the division of the way, cross a footbridge over a stream and take the right branch. Follow the path as it continues, with the stream to the right, and low cliffs, ablaze with gorse, to the left. Then the path narrows and becomes quite delightful, with sedge warblers calling from the bushes. Iris, kingcup, primrose and cowslip colour the verges in spring. The rising path continues and the little burn moves away right and flows through a tortuous narrow ravine.

2 As you reach the brow, the magnificent, extensive ruined Slains castle (no entry) comes into view. Walk on towards it and then wind a little right to see the outer wall, dropping sheer to a rocky bay. Return and follow the main track left, past a poignant memorial stone, just in front of the castle. Stride on along the track beside the inlet of Long Haven, a huge ravine that must have given the castle protection from attack on this side. Continue up the walled track, which probably once gave access to the castle, and follow it as it swings right.

3 At the cross of tracks, bear right to walk a wide long way that passes through vast arable fields from where, in summer, you are constantly serenaded by skylarks. At the track end go through a small parking area and wind right through a gate and on along a fine grassy path, hedged with gorse, back towards the sea. Then bear left to begin a magical walk along the grassy sward, also part of the coastal way, where care should be taken as the path comes close to the edge of some very steep, sheer, magnificent cliffs. There is a fence on your left side but not on the cliff edge side. Ahead stand the island of Dunbuy and the headland of Grey Mare. Look for the huge hole high up in a wall of rock through which fly a stream of seabirds. Every suitable ledge has its kittiwake, fulmar, cormorant, or razorbill nesting in spring. Rock doves fly out of dark crevices in the

Razorbill

cliff, swallows twitter from the fence wire and sand martins fly overhead, a fascinating spot for birdwatchers.

4 At the fence corner, wind round a large cove on a narrow path, very high up and close to the edge. If you wish to view the birds, stand still to enjoy them. Continue on and at the next fence corner, take the path, left, up beside it. At the Y-junction of paths, take the right branch, keeping to the right of a solitary post. The path, now greatly improved, curves left and

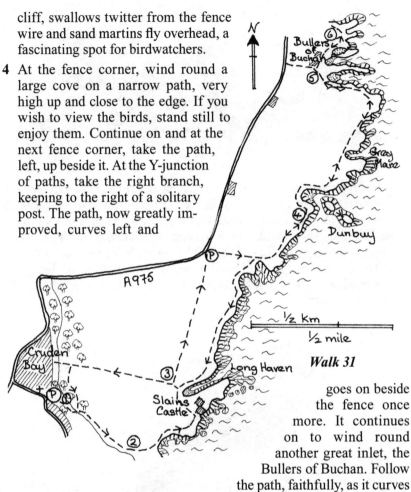

Walk 31

goes on beside the fence once more. It continues on to wind round another great inlet, the Bullers of Buchan. Follow the path, faithfully, as it curves left, still beside the fence, beside smaller inlets of the cove. Again the path is narrow, and often comes to the cliff edge and could be slippery after rain. Pause to look across the Bullers to see a magnificent arch, the Bow of Pitwartlachie, through which the sea pours.

5 The way then descends to the settlement. Walk, right, in front of the several cottages and then continue up the coastal path to an information board, beside a great hole in the cliff, called The Pot. It was once a large sea cave before its roof fell in on the floor of the sea below.

6 To return, retrace your steps along the cliff path until you reach the end of the grassy path, hedged with gorse, at point 3. Ignore this right turn and go on ahead on a grassy path. Cross two footbridges and carry

Sea Campion

on with a fence to your right, to arrive at a purpose built gap onto the walled track, with the castle to your left. Turn right and where the track swings right, take a walled track on the left, which goes down between fields and enters a wood, where you take a path that goes off left. Walk along the edge of a field on the well beaten path. Follow it as it swings left and descends a bank to join the outward track, at the bridge, taken at the outset of the walk. Turn right to walk a short way through the trees to the car park.

Skylark

Practicals

Type of walk: Excellent, but take care on the cliffs.

Complete distance:	5½ miles/9km
Time:	3 hours
Maps:	OS Explorer 427/Landranger 30

32

Loch of Strathbeg

Park in St. Combs, in East Street, near the toilets and cemetery, grid ref 056633, or turn right towards the Tufted Duck Hotel and park on the left before you reach it, taking care not to block the entrance to a house, grid ref 057629. If you park here you should walk back into the village and turn right into East Street. To access St. Combs take the B9033, which leaves the A90 at the south end of Fraserburgh and joins it again about 2 miles west of Crimond.

In the first half of the 19th century **St Combs** was a prosperous herring-fishing village. Local fishermen, earning a lot of money, squandered it on whisky. Their families lived in crude hovels and rubbish piled up in the streets. But all this changed after two severe cholera

Distant Rattray Head

epidemics ravaged the village. Its cottages, built gable-end to the sea to help withstand the gales, are now holiday retreats.

The **Loch of Strathbeg** was formed after a terrible sand storm around 1720, which also destroyed the little port of Rattray at the southern end of Strathbeg Bay. The reed-fringed loch attracts thousands of birds, many over wintering, others migrating here in the spring and autumn. It is now a RSPB reserve.

1 From East Street walk down the track to the right of the cemetery and join another sandy track running behind the dunes with a steep grassy cliff to your right. The path divides but rejoins; choose the one that runs nearest to the shore and gives the best views. Notice an old winch for winding boats in up the shore where the stones have been cleared. Many waders such as ringed plovers, dunlin and turnstones frequent the rocky shore.

2 Cross a track and walk ahead on a small path, which goes over a ditch on a plank bridge, then winds right round the base of the dunes. There are northern marsh orchids in the damper places and the ground is blue with dune pansies in summer; rabbits scatter in all directions at any time of year. Follow the path for over a mile until it runs down to a footbridge over a deep ditch. Cross and go through the gate on the other side. Walk left and cross a gated bridge over the outflow from the loch, then follow a grassy track up a bank to the right.

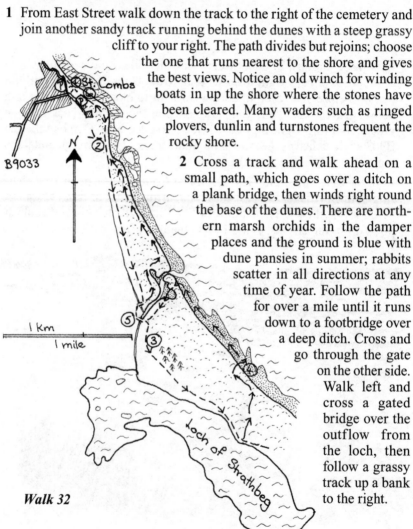

Walk 32

106

3 Head for a group of conifers and go round the right side of the trees. Pause to enjoy the view over the loch, which is home to many hundreds of geese, swans and ducks in winter, and terns in summer. Continue along the track for about another ¾ mile/1.1km as it comes closer to the water of the loch and gives good views. Then wind left to cross the several lines of dunes towards the sea, using animal tracks to help you through the marram. At a wide low level area (dune slack), walk north along it until you can take a track winding over the top of the last line of dunes and continuing down to the shore.

Curlew

4 Turn left and walk along the beach, enjoying the waves and the wind. Look out to sea for gulls, terns and gannets, and you may spot arctic skuas. If the tide is low you can walk round the end of the dunes where the burn (crossed earlier) comes out across a wide sandy inlet. At high spring tides this will be under water so in these conditions you will need to return up over the dunes well before you reach the burn and make your way round the head of the inlet. A sandy track leads along the burn at the other side of the burn back to the bridges.

5 Cross the bridges and then follow a line of old fence posts towards the shore, where a track runs along the top of the dunes. Where they bend right, go down and cross the pansy-strewn dune slack, then climb back to the ridge and follow the crest (or the alternative path just below it), with splendid views over the shore out to Rattray Head lighthouse. As you approach St. Combs the shore becomes rockier, with sandy pools where common seals haul out on the enclosing rocks. The dunes get lower and the path comes down and winds left to the plank bridge.

Dune Pansies

6 Follow your outward path to return to your car. As you reach the village three paths branch, left, off the main track at the same point; take the third which heads towards the cemetery (unless you have left your car on the clifftop, in which case take whichever is most appropriate.)

Arctic Skua chasing Tern

Practicals

Type of walk: Level, mainly easy walking. The part where you cross the dunes is pathless but you can hear the sea to help with direction finding. Watch out for rabbit holes. Be aware of the tide, although you are not likely to be cut off by it.

Complete distance: 7½ miles/12km
Time: 4–5 hours
Maps: OS Explorer 427/Landranger 30

Troup Head RSPB Reserve

Park in the small car park, grid ref 823664. To access this leave the A98 about 1 mile/1.5km south-east of MacDuff by the B9031, signed to Gardenstown and Pennan. Drive past the turns for Gardenstown and Crovie and look for a RSPB sign for Troup Head Reserve. Turn right at the first junction and follow small discreet signs to Northfield farm. Here turn left and drive through the farmyard, then right down a reinforced track between fields to the small car park.

Troup Head is 350ft/106m high. It is home to Scotland's only mainland gannet colony, which is part of the 150,000 seabirds that use every available rock ledge. The cliff faces are alive with guillemot, razorbill, puffin, kittiwake and fulmar.

View east from Troup Head

1 Continue along the track from the car park. Go through the first gate, signed and arrowed, on the right. Pass through the next gate and stroll

along the top edge of a field. From here there are fine views, east, over Pennan Bay. At a gate gap, take the right fork leading uphill between banks of gorse. Look for wheatears and you may spot a hare here. A grassy track crosses the one you are on, and you bear right on this, down to a small gate giving access to the cliff top. Notices warn you that it is unprotected.

Walk 33a

2 Go ahead on a small path to a viewing area from where you can see cliffs with hundreds of kittiwake, guillemot, fulmars and razorbills. Then return to the gate and climb arrowed steps. Cross the hilltop and go down the far side, passing a gate which is your return path.

3 Carry on along the path to a view-point. You might wish to lie down against a raised bank here, to enjoy the magnificent view of the gannet colony. Watching the gannets fly in and out, interacting with each other is superb. Bird watchers will want to spend a long time here, but don't forget your binoculars. Out to sea you can see rafts of auks.

Gannet

4 When you wish to move on, continue on the path, just by the fence, to a notice which tells you that it is the end of the RSBP

trail. Go on a few steps for a splendid view west along the coast, but the clifftop is rather overgrown beyond this. Retrace your steps to go through the gate noted on the way down and follow the grassy path round the hillside, until it joins your outward path. Return to the car park.

Hare

Practicals

Type of walk: Amazing for all birders. Enjoy the magic site, with care.

Complete distance: 1 mile
Time: As long as you can spare
Maps: OS Explorer 426/Landranger 29 or 30

33b

The Tore of Troup

Park at the track end in a large car park above Cullykhan Bay, grid ref 835661. To access this, drive along B9031, which leaves the A98 just outside (south-east of) MacDuff, until a mile before Pennan. Turn left along a track signed to car park.

Pennan is a picturesque fishing village on the east coast of Scotland. It has rich red sandstone cliffs, shingle, rocks and cottages, that all glow in sunshine. Most dwellings are end-on to the sea separated from the beach just by a road. There is a small attractive harbour. It lies at the end of a steep zigzagging road where the cottages are backed by a high sheer wall of rock. Pennan Head ends in 350ft/106m high cliffs, which provide nesting sites for puffin, guillemot, razorbill and also house martins.

Pennan

Cullykhan Bay is a secluded cliff-sheltered sandy cove with a rocky, shingle, and sandy beach crossed by Jacobshall Burn.

1 Go left out of the entrance of the car park down a path signed to Fort Fiddes. This crosses a very narrow neck of land onto the rocky promontory of Castle Point, where you can see the grassed remains of the ramparts of the ancient fort. Follow the path round inside the fence and enjoy the splendid views of cliffs and Lion's Head, and across to Pennan nestling in its tiny bay. Kittiwakes and fulmars soar past. The huge hole in the headland opposite is called Hell's Lum (chimney); it is a collapsed cave, but there is no access. Then return to the car park, which you leave to continue the walk by the way you entered.

2 Immediately, turn right through a gate, to walk along another track into trees. Keep left at a junction and follow the top of the wood, past a house with an attractive duckpond, to a junction by a bungalow. Turn right here, back into the wood. At the next junction go left onto an access road, where there is a pond on the right. Continue out to the main road, where you turn left, and 220yds/200m, along, turn right past the Old Doctor's House, onto a metalled road which soon becomes a reinforced track. It winds left and then right, slanting along the hillside into the hidden valley of the Tore of Troup. Go through a gate and on through woodland and then pastures, with increasingly delightful views. The path gradually descends through mature deciduous trees to the valley bottom, with the Tore Burn to the left. Go on to cross a tributary burn to reach an area of farm sheds and slurry pits. Turn sharply left and cross the Tore Burn on a bridge.

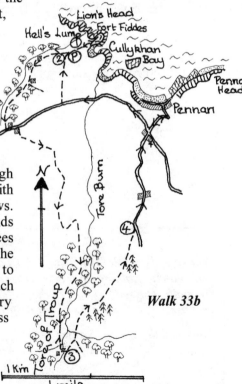

Walk 33b

3 Go through a gate and uphill. Where the path bends right in a hairpin,

go straight ahead on a rather less obvious track. Cross a small burn in a ravine on stones and follow the track across fields; at first it is not very clear as it runs through gorse but there are many alternative paths which all, eventually, come together. The farmer keeps cows in the pastures and the track may be very muddy in wet weather. Go past a ruined building and on up the hill on a much clearer track below a conifer wood, then finally out onto a minor road at the top of the hill.

4 Turn left and walk down it until you reach the main road. Cross to the opposite side and walk carefully downhill into the village of Pennan, with its dwellings end-on to the sea. At high tide it seems as if the sea might be coming into the houses. Turn right to look at the tiny harbour, or left, to the raised viewpoint. Then return up the steep hill to the main road. Turn right and walk down into the valley, then up the far side to the track to the car park above Cullykhan Bay. If you still have any energy left you may like to take the stepped path out of the far end of the car park, which goes down to the lovely sandy bay, but you have to return by the same route.

Kittiwake

Practicals

Type of walk: Mainly on clear tracks and minor roads. Some unavoidable walking on a B-road. Very steep down to Pennan and up again. The second part of the valley, after crossing the burn, was well used by cows but they kept their distance.

Complete distance:	5 miles/8km
Time:	3 hours
Maps:	OS Explorer 426/Landranger 29

114

34

River Deveron at Banff

Park in the pay and display car park in Banff's very grand square overlooked by the Visitor Centre, grid ref 689637.

Terraced streets rise quite steeply from the harbour at **Banff**, which was the focal point of this ancient county town until the herring boom ended in the 1920s. The new marina, opened in 2007, accommodates over 60 yachts. Part of this walk passes through the woodland of **Duff House**, the fine Georgian mansion built in 1735, by the architect, William Adam as a seat for the Earls of Fife. The River Deveron flows through the grounds, eventually reaching Banff by flowing under the seven-arched bridge, built by John Smeaton in 1772, which links Banff with Macduff.

Banff Bridge

It is said that **James Duff MP**, was so intensely proud of his Scottish birth and ancestry that he had Banffshire soil shipped to London and spread in his garden at Old Whitehill Palace, where he was building a house. He could then say that it was sited on Scottish soil. He eventually became the 2nd Earl of Fife.

Walk 34

1 Leave the square, south-west, to cross the very busy main road. Descend the access track, signed for the car park for Duff House. Where the track divides into three, go ahead on the one to the right. Pass through the large 18th century gates into glorious deciduous woodland. A few steps along turn left to take the 'alternative path' through Wrack Wood, which bends and curves through beech, horsechestnut and wych elm. In early spring the woodland floor is a mass of snowdrops contrasting sharply with the leaves of wood rush. These pretty flowers are followed by a carpet of bluebells. At a signpost you may wish to visit the ice house, an underground chamber filled with ice, the 18th century 'refrigerator' for Duff House. Return to the alternative path and continue on the lovely way. Go past a stubby headstone, commemorating Victorian pets and walk on to reach the mausoleum, built in the Gothic style, in 1791, which includes a memorial to the 1st Earl of Fife. The mausoleum stands at a glorious bend in the River Deveron. At this point the alternative path and the main path, come together and they continue as a track. Here the Aberdeenshire Council access agreement through the woodland ceases.

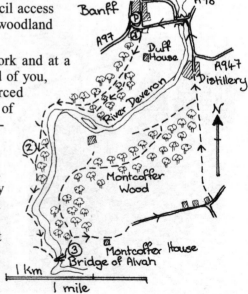

2 Bear right at the next fork and at a modern bungalow ahead of you, keep left. The reinforced way runs along the edge of wood, with mixed farmland stretching away to the right. Pass through great banks of gorse and then on under some lovely beeches, where you can see far down to the river. Descend gently left towards it to cross the bridge of Alvah. This stretches high above

116

the River Deveron, firmly anchored on the spectacular crags on either side of the waterway. It was built by Lord Fife to link his properties on both banks of the river.

3 Ignore the gate ahead and turn left uphill. Continue on the now narrow metalled way to pass Montcoffer House (private) once part of the Dukes of Fife estate. Carry on for almost 1 mile/1.7km, passing the Mains of Montcoffer, to reach a road junction at Montcoffer Lodge. Turn left and, after a few steps, turn sharp left and follow the footpath into Montcoffer Wood, where you are most likely to spot red squirrels. Go over the hill, through the lovely deciduous woodland and then descend a track, running ahead, keeping straight, with farmland to the left. Go on along the metalled way to pass through the buildings of Macduff distillery and on to join the main road. Cross the bridge and follow the road to reach the car park on the far side.

Red Squirrel

Practicals

Type of walk: This a lovely ramble at all times of the year, mainly on reinforced tracks, paths and narrow roads.

Complete distance:	6 miles/10km
Time:	3 hours
Maps:	OS Explorer 426 & 425/Landranger 29

35

Portsoy via Sandend
to Findlater Castle

Park in the square at Portsoy, grid ref 588665. The village lies on the A98, about 9 miles west of Banff and east of Buckie.

Portsoy stands on a rocky promontory and lies on the north-east coast of Scotland approximately 55 miles north-west of Aberdeen. It is an old fishing village with a picturesque 17th century harbour, unusual in that its walls were constructed with vertical stone rather than horizontal; it also has a more modern outer harbour. It is famous for its annual Scottish Traditional Boat Festival.

Portsoy marble is really polished serpentine. It was used for two magnificent chimney pieces in Versailles for Louis XIV. Today many delightful curios, using the pink or green rock, are sold in the Portsoy Marble showroom by the harbour.

Portsoy Harbour

Findlater Castle stands on a promontory 150ft/50m high and guarded on three sides by sheer sea-washed cliffs. Built in the 15th century by the Ogilvie family it was abandoned around 1600. It can be viewed from the circular viewpoint and can be reached, with care, on foot along a spine of grassy rock.

1 From the Square at Portsoy, walk down North High Street, past fine stone houses and several restored buildings, soon to reach the harbour. Spend time here enjoying this lovely corner. Then return a few steps up the street to take a track, on the right, signed Coastal Trail, a white on brown sign with an anchor on it. Carry on a fenced path along the cliffs, to look down on the sea far below. Away to the left stretch huge arable fields. As you go ignore any paths dropping down to the delightful coves on the shore.

2 The good track then moves inland, passing through vast areas of gorse. Look and listen for linnets, twites and skylarks here. The next waymark directs you, right, along a grassy track that leads back to the cliff edge, the diversion taking you safely round a large inlet of the sea.

3 Once beyond a ruined small building and some rusting winding gear, take the signed right branch to walk on the lovely way to the point. From here you can look across an

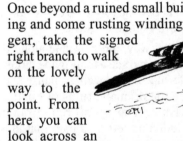

Twite

extensive bay to Sandend village. Away to the left stands the Bin of Cullen, a wooded hill, 1063ft/326m high, from where there is a magnificent view. Return a few steps from the cliff edge, and then continue on the high-level cliff path, along the east side of Sandend Bay, with treacherous jagged rocks below.

4 Descend, steadily, to a gate, with steps beyond. Ford the burn of Fordyce and, if the tide is low, stroll, right, across the glorious sands. If the tide is in, wind right behind the concrete blocks of wartime defences and climb up one of the narrow paths onto the grassy dunes at the back of the beach. Walk on along the continuing path, towards the village, to cross a bridge over the burn on its way to cross the sands.

5 Wind round the edge of a caravan park to join the road at Sandend, a

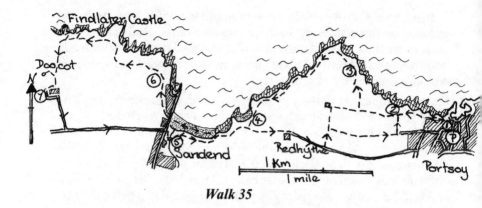

Walk 35

small village strung out along the western shore of Sandend Bay and then walk right to an older part of the village. Here many of the picturesque houses stand head on to the sea to withstand the North Sea winds. Stroll the pleasing harbour and then return along the road for a short way, to take on the right, a concrete access track, which soon curves uphill and is signed 'Coastal footpath to Sunnyside Beach'. As you near the house above, take, on the right, a well signed narrow footpath that traverses a grassy slope above the roof tops of the houses about the harbour, from where there are excellent views.

6 Beyond the stile, turn left onto a grassy way and continue along the pleasing, gently climbing path. When you can see a man-made circular structure, the viewpoint for the castle, ahead on the cliffs, pause at the waymark before it. Look right to see the dramatic ruins of Findlater Castle. Some walkers will wish to visit it. If so, set off right from the waymark, then almost immediately descend left on a path that looks more difficult than it is, and follow the path as it curves right and leads up to the Castle rock. Return the same way to turn right on the main path. In a few steps take a wide track, left, leading away from the sea. This track brings you to a parking area behind the fire damaged Barnyards of Findlater.

7 Follow the track as it bears left and then follow it, right, downhill. At the T-junction go left and walk downhill for ½ mile to reach the road that passes through Sandend. Cross and retrace your steps over the footbridge. Walk east over the sands, or along the dunes. Wade the Fordyce Burn and follow the little path to re-climb the steps. Ascend the path to the top of the cliff to reach a waymark beside a fence. Walk the 'green trail', right, and pass to the left of Redhythe farm. The track then becomes a tarmac road. Take the first farm track, on the left and,

120

220yds/200m along, stride a grassy track, right, between banks of gorse. Carry straight on towards Portsoy and at the end of the track, turn left along a road to rejoin your outward path. Turn right and walk back to the harbour. Turn right up North High Street to return to the Square.

Gorse

Practicals

Type of walk: Delightful, with wonderful views, but not to be attempted in a strong wind. The first part along the high cliffs is best attempted in walking gear. Children and dogs must be under close control.

Complete distance:	6–7 miles/9.5–11km
Time:	3–4 hours
Maps:	OS Explorer 425/Landranger 29

36

Bin of Cullen from Old Cullen

Park in Cullen in a large car park at the end of the road, grid ref 508664. To access this, leave the square in the centre of Cullen by Grant Street and turn left up South Deskford Street before reaching the gates of Cullen House. Follow the signs for Cullen Kirk. Turn right and right again and drive to the end of the road.

Look for **Oak Fern** in sheltered, shady places. It has thin delicate fronds that shrivel easily in sunshine or wind, though it is quite happy growing in dry situations where the rootstock will be free of moisture. It grows well on mountain sides and in Scotland may reach an altitude of 3000ft/900m. It can be recognised by its triple frond and when the plant is fully-grown it is four to six inches high. It is a brighter green than most ferns. It does not survive well the earliest frosts.

Cullen Old Kirk

Bin is a corruption into Scots of the Gaelic word for hill 'beinn' There are several 'bins' in the Moray plain, all isolated significant hills. The Bin of Cullen is the most dramatic, being near the coast and visible from a long way off in all directions.

1 Walk on from the end of the road, with an area of mown grass to your left and a wall to your right, along a rather overgrown but still used path. Where it emerges onto a metalled drive, with imposing gates and lodges to your right, cross and go along the track opposite, still beside a wall. Carry on past some ruins and then through a gate gap in the wall into the woodlands of Cullen House.

At a track junction, by a house, turn sharp right round a barrier and stroll through superb mature trees with the Burn of Deskford to your left. Cross the burn on the track then, where it makes a hairpin bend, go left along a less well-used track that runs beside the Glen Burn. At the Y-junction keep left. The track keeps to the fairly level ground by the burn, rising gradually through mixed woodland. After a dark area of Sitka Spruce, the path climbs into more open pine forest, where oak fern grows beside the path.

Walk 36

2 At a cross of paths go straight ahead, uphill, through lovely open woodland. Keep on ascending until the path levels out at the col between the Bin and the Little Bin, where you turn left on a clear path. This zigzags gently through twisted pine trees, which become smaller and lower as you get higher until they are only a few feet high. Do not use the short cut paths, which are steeper and have become very eroded. The views open out as you go; there is a splendid panorama of the Moray Coast across to Morven in Sutherland, and inland to Ben Rinnes and Tap

o'Noth. At the summit is a cairn and a view indicator, where you will want to pause.

3 Return by the same route to the col and turn left along the continuation of the path you came up. Walk right at a Y-junction and go downhill through open forest, past an area of beech trees and then through pine. At a T-junction, turn left and carry on downhill. Ignore a track going left, then at the end of a fenced area take the right turn at another T-junction. This track winds through a hollow and soon runs down to a well-used track. Turn right and continue down the valley with a burn to the right among the trees, then cross the burn on a stone bridge and bear left at the next junction.

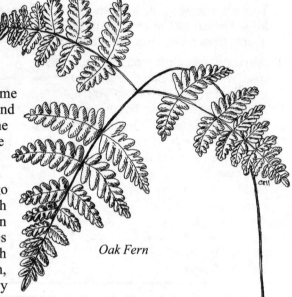

Oak Fern

4 This track eventually emerges from the trees into fields. Cross a major track and walk down a path, lined by ash trees, between fields of cereal crops. At the end bear right to join a metalled road, then in a few metres, fork left onto another reinforced track. This runs along above the valley of the Burn of Deskford to the hairpin bend where you left it on your outward path. Retrace your steps to the car park. If you have time you may like to walk down the broad road to visit the old kirk; it is not

Roe Deer

always open but it is very interesting to wander round the graveyard with its carved gravestones, and peep through the big window to see the galleried interior. Rumour has it that the gallery was built to keep the smelly fishermen away from the richer people (from Cullen House).

Pine Marten

Practicals

Type of walk: Good paths, with some climbing.

Complete distance: 8 miles/13km
Time: 3–4 hours
Maps: OS Explorer 425/Landranger 29

37

Cullen to Portknockie

Park in the middle of Cullen, grid ref 513673. If driving west along the A98, the parking area and toilets lie off to the right side (east) of the road.

Cullen was built in the 19th century by the Earl of Seafield, whose family owned 16th century Cullen House (itself built by Ogilvies in 1600), set in wooded parkland, a mile from the sea. The harbour at Seatown is Cullen's old fishing quarter. The mile long sandy beach is backed by golf links and cradled by craggy headlands.

The **Countess of Seafield** would not allow the railway to run through the policies of her estate and so the 19th century engineers had to re-route the line through the town and over spectacular viaducts. Look for the **Temple of Pomona,** just before the viaduct on your

Bowfiddle Rock

return. It was built in the shape of a classical temple and used as a tea-house by the folk at Cullen House. Today the house has been converted into luxury homes.

Portknockie has the best natural harbour on the Moray Firth's southern shore. Fishermen moved to the village from the 17th century onwards. Quays and a breakwater were built and the village became a centre for the herring fishing industry. Once the latter moved to the bigger ports such as Aberdeen Portknockie on its high rocky headland was left with only its memories and its spectacular **Bowfiddle Rock arch**.

1 Walk down the main street, pass under the fine arch of the old railway line, which frames a grand seascape and continue across a large grassy area, with dramatic views from here of the viaduct, and ahead to the harbour, where you will want to pause. Then bear left towards the viaduct to go past the houses of Seatown, the rows of houses end on to the sea. Go on to cross the Burn of Cullen and continue past the three stacks, known as the Three Kings, which interrupt the glorious arc of Cullen Sands.

2 Continue along the beach. If the tide is in, and the sands are covered, you will need to walk on the footpath that runs along the top of a low boulder clay barrier along the edge of the golf course. Go past a huge outcrop of conglomerate rock, which glows a warm red in the sunshine. Carry on towards the gorse-covered cliffs ahead. At the far-top corner of the beach, or at the end of the footpath along the barrier, bear right along a little path that takes you on round the foot of the cliffs and behind rocks. If the tide is very high this might cause a problem. Away to your right is a chaos of reefs, rocky outcrops stretching finger-like out to sea. Wind round a short way to reach a fine cave where a good path starts again.

3 Climb on round the base of the next cliff on a narrow well-made path just above the high tide level. There is a spring here, called Jenny's Well. Pass a marker post with the name 'Portknockie' on it and ascend the steadily rising path up the sheer cliff. To your right are fantastic rock shapes. Then climb several sandstone steps from where there is a superb view of a huge cave. Go on up the now concreted path, climb-ing more steps to reach a bench seat, where you might want to pause. Continue on up the path to the top of the cliff. Here a grassy path turns left to the edge of Portknockie—but this walk continues on round the headland on an unsigned narrow but good path.

4 Pass an information board, which tells you about the famous Bowfiddle

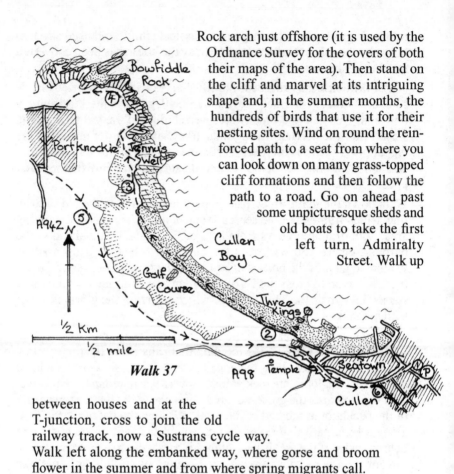

Rock arch just offshore (it is used by the Ordnance Survey for the covers of both their maps of the area). Then stand on the cliff and marvel at its intriguing shape and, in the summer months, the hundreds of birds that use it for their nesting sites. Wind on round the reinforced path to a seat from where you can look down on many grass-topped cliff formations and then follow the path to a road. Go on ahead past some unpicturesque sheds and old boats to take the first left turn, Admiralty Street. Walk up

Walk 37

between houses and at the
T-junction, cross to join the old
railway track, now a Sustrans cycle way.
Walk left along the embanked way, where gorse and broom flower in the summer and from where spring migrants call.

Common Seals

5 Suddenly you have a fine view, steeply down to the golf course and the beach below. There are seats at this viewpoint to enjoy it all. Carry on along the grand high-level promenade to the next pair of seats and look down on the grand vista once more. Then continue to just before the magnificent curving viaduct and look right to see the temple on its grassy hillock above woodland. Stride the viaduct from where tall walkers will enjoy the view of the harbour, the town and further bridges along the defunct railway track.

6 Beyond the viaduct move on to cross a single arched bridge and, at its end, turn sharp right down the route taken by cyclists and continue up a quiet residential street. Bear left along Grant Street and cross the main road to reach the car park.

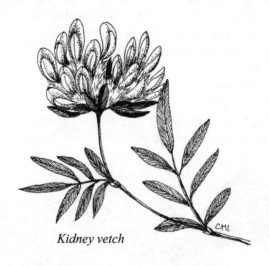

Kidney vetch

Practicals

Type of walk: Very pleasing. Some people might find the path to Portknockie a little vertiginous and children and dogs should be under very firm control. Take note of the tide as you round the short way below the cliffs.

Complete distance:	5 miles/8km
Time:	3–4 hours
Maps:	OS Explorer 425/Landranger 29

38

Spey Bay, Garmouth, and the Lein

Park in the large car park by the old ice house at the end of the road in Tugnet, grid ref 348654. To access this take the B9104, which leaves the A96 (Keith to Elgin) road, east of the bridge over the Spey, between Fochabers and Mosstodloch. Drive to the end of the road.

The **water tower** was built in 19th century to provide a clean water supply for Kingston and Garmouth and was an early concrete construction.

The **standing stones** are of a type called a 4-poster from about 1500 BC and are thought to be a burial ground.

Kingston and Garmouth had a thriving ship-building industry from 1785, when the first yard was opened, until the end of the

Water Tower and Standing Stones, Garmouth

19th century. In its heyday there were 7 shipyards. They built timber ships using wood that was floated down the Spey from the forests of Glenmore and Upper Speyside. Kingston was formerly called Port of Garmouth but was renamed after Kingston-on-Hull where the main owners of the shipbuilding business came from.

The **ice-house at Tugnet** is the largest in Scotland and was built for storing salmon.

The Spey is a daunting river, wide and fast flowing, and it washes vast quantities of gravel down from its mountain catchment. There are stony islands, many braided channels, and many uprooted trees that have also been washed down.

1 Go up to the front of the ice-house behind the car park and look out to sea. You may see the Moray Firth bottlenose dolphins, which often frequent this area. Then continue past the Wildlife Centre to turn left on a road above an inlet, running in front of several houses. Follow a Speyside Way sign, which directs you right. The path follows the edge of the estuary, which can be quite exciting at high tide and high wind. Look in the fields on the left for flocks of yellowhammers and linnets, and listen for skylarks singing. To your right, the water is soon replaced by reeds and then wet woodland with alder and pussy willow. Ignore a path on the right.

Bottlenose Dolphin

2 At a cross of paths do not take the first right but go uphill onto the old railway bed, now a surfaced cycle track, and walk right, with woodland on both sides. Ahead is the old railway viaduct over the Spey, a dramatic structure; it is worth going down steps to a small platform, below the end of the bridge, for a fine view along it.

3 Cross the viaduct and walk on until a road bridge crosses above the track; climb steps on the left to it and walk, right, over the bridge

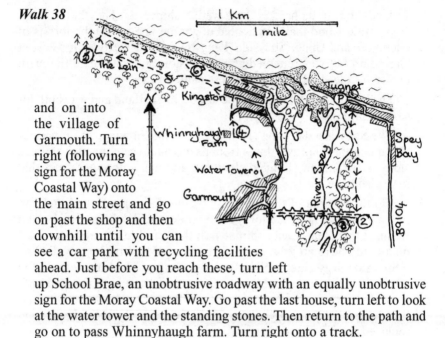

and on into the village of Garmouth. Turn right (following a sign for the Moray Coastal Way) onto the main street and go on past the shop and then downhill until you can see a car park with recycling facilities ahead. Just before you reach these, turn left up School Brae, an unobtrusive roadway with an equally unobtrusive sign for the Moray Coastal Way. Go past the last house, turn left to look at the water tower and the standing stones. Then return to the path and go on to pass Whinnyhaugh farm. Turn right onto a track.

4 The track then turns into a metalled road that bends right. Here take a footpath on the left. Cross a bridge over a burn and walk between houses to a road. Turn left and continue to its end. Wind right round the garden wall of the last house to go down a pebble bank and head on along a distinct path. Cross a track, then bear left at a junction. Follow the main path over open heath, and then through low birch and pine woodland.

5 Turn right where the path joins a wider track to cross shingle ridges, with a low scrub of burnet rose and juniper edging the way. At its end, walk right on another wide track. This goes along behind the shingle bank all the way back to Kingston. As you go look over the shingle at intervals to the sea where you might spot gannets, terns and mergansers in summer, and in winter, scoter, velvet scoters, long tailed duck and eiders. You might also see ospreys fishing in summer.

Long-tailed Ducks

6 At a large car park keep left along the back of the shingle. Walk outside a recreation ground and then to the left of houses, with a sea inlet to your left, until you reach a car park. Turn right through it and join the road to walk back to Garmouth along the sandy path by the road with the estuary to your left. Rejoin your outward path in Garmouth and walk back to Tugnet.

Burnet Rose

Practicals	
Type of walk: Level ramble on good tracks and paths. Lots to see.	
Complete distance:	7 miles/11.4km
Time:	3–4 hours
Maps:	OS Explorer 424/Landranger 28

39

Burghead to Hopeman

Park in the car park at Burghead, grid ref 111689. To access this, take a left turn off the B9089, just before a memorial statue, at a Y-junction, signposted 'Harbour Master's Office and Toilets'. The car park lies against the sea wall of the harbour.

Burghead is built on most of the site of what was once the capital of the northern Picts. It has orderly ranks of 19th century houses lining a

Natural arch near Hopeman

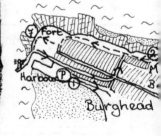

stubby headland, with a sandy beach backed by sand dunes. On the tip of the headland stand the remains of a Pictish fort, almost completely lost when, in 1805, a fishing village was destroyed to make way for present buildings and to extend the harbour. Today it is a pleasant place to sit on one of several benches overlooking the remains of the now tranquil fort to enjoy the sun and the sea.

On January 11 (except if that date is a Sunday and then the event occurs on January 10) the annual festival of **Burning of the Clavie** takes place, an ancient pagan fire ceremony. The Clavie is a barrel filled with wood and tar and then set alight before being carried around the streets of Burghead by the Clavie King.

Hopeman was also built in the 19th century. It has a small sandy beach but to the west of the village is a rocky shore. Its high cliffs are pitted with caves and quarries, which have given up fossils of many prehistoric reptiles.

Almost at the start of this walk Burghead is dominated by the huge **maltings** building which was erected in 1966, then extended in 1971 to double production. This is where the grain used in the production of whisky is prepared, and can be described as the real start of the famous 'Whisky Trail' which winds its way through Moray.

1   Return inland to the Y-junction as directed by a sign for the 'Moray Coast Footpath'. Cross the main road and walk ahead. Go over several smaller turnings and, where the road swings sharp left, go ahead to join the coast path. Turn right to pass in front of the maltings. Once past the latter, carry on through a gate and go on along the track of the dismantled railway (a Beeching cut).

2   Stroll the delightful way as it runs above the shore through the lovely countryside, below sloping cliffs and through cuttings, lined with gorse. As you go you have wonderful glimpses of the shore down below the cliffs, with

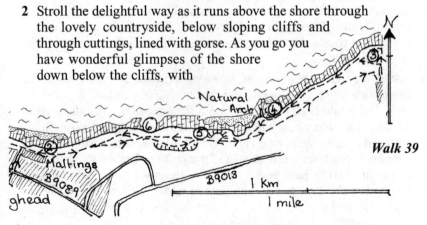

Walk 39

135

rocky outcrops, stacks and reefs from where many birds come and go. About the edge of the track, look for meadow saxifrage, scurvy grass and thrift and listen for whitethroat, yellow hammer, twite and linnet. Pass through a large flat open area, an old quarry, then on under a bridge to walk through a magnificent cutting. Pass under a second bridge. Carry on towards the village of Hopeman. Where the next bridge blocks your way, climb steps, on the right, to cross above the track. Walk ahead over rough vegetation, with a caravan park to your right, to a seat overlooking the glorious shore. This is the place for your first break.

3 Then begin your return. Walk back towards the bridge you crossed and half way along the path, turn right on a narrow but distinct path, through gorse. Note the great sandstone boulders on the shore and the long fingers of rock that push out into the sea, a haven for kittiwakes and other gulls. Follow the easy path, where more gorse stretches inland to the left, and with the sea just below you to the right. The path then leads down to the beach, a mass of rounded boulders. Walk on as others have done along the foot of the cliffs. If

Meadow Saxifrage

the weather, or the tide have changed, you may need to move over, left, to the railway track. As the cliff curves round, a short path leaves the boulders and moves up a slope and then it drops down again to continue, easily, along the bouldery shore. The way becomes wide and grassy and passes through a large open area, leading up a slope away from the shore.

4 Just before a green marker post, take a right turn to descend towards the shore once more. Continue round the curving bay to look at a natural arch. If the tide is right, pass through the arch to see the sheer cliffs beyond, with a tiny beach in front of a huge cave. Go back through the arch and climb a short way, right, to visit another fascinating cave. To continue, return for a few steps and then take either the stepped path, or a rising narrow path beside the gorse, to return to the railway track just before the first bridge you passed under earlier. Turn right, go under the bridge and continue on past the next bay, where you might spot youngsters climbing a huge sea stack.

5 Carry on a short way on the track to come to the quarry and take a narrow path (the line of the original track) that carries on very close to the edge of the cliffs. Here sand martins nest in holes below you. The path is a delight. When you reach a small path off, left, take it if you have young children with you, because the path deteriorates as it continues. The views from the path are splendid but stand still to enjoy them.

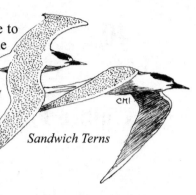

Sandwich Terns

6 At the start of the next cutting, take another narrow path off right. At first it climbs a little, then descends to becomes a good grassy way leading to a seat from where you can enjoy more views of the birds and of the sea. Then go on past the maltings, and walk ahead on the continuing track, with cottages lying back to your left beyond a grassy area with picnic tables. Continue on the now metalled way to come to a sign directing you left for the Pictish fort, a large open grassy space, with high ground to the left and right. Walk up the left turn and then take steps on the right to enjoy seats overlooking the hollow, with the sea ahead and the sea behind you. After a pause, walk on to the visitor centre, housed in what is probably the base of an old lighthouse. Climb the steps to the top for a superb view across the Moray Firth

7 Stroll on along the grassy path, which heads towards the outer break-waters of the harbour. Go down old worn narrow sandstone steps to a lower level. Turn right and carry on down a ramp to a large sandstone outcrop. Turn left again and descend concrete steps, with a chain fastened to the side wall to help you down. Walk along the side of the harbour. Turn right at the sign on the first building, an old granary designed by Telford, and on down to walk back to the car park.

Practicals

Type of walk: Very satisfactory. Enjoy the old railway track and the return along the shoreline, which is mainly rocks and pebbles, with an opportunity to find hidden caves. The sea is not safe for swimming.

Complete distance: 5–6 miles/8–10km
Time: 4 hours
Maps: OS Explorer 423/Landranger 28

40

Culbin Forest

Park in the Wellhill Forestry Commission car park, grid ref 997614. To access this leave the A96 one mile west of Forres and follow minor roads signed to Kintessack and Culbin.

The route up **Hill 99** makes it an easy climb and suitable for most walkers. The tower at the top, a wonderful wooden structure, known as the 'squirrel's eye' viewpoint, gives you a splendid view over the forest and out to the Moray Firth. The tower is constructed on sand, using sand-filled car tyres, which buttress the approach ramp to the 46ft/15m long walkway. The tyres were easy to transport and caused minimal impact on Culbin's fragile environment. The safe and long lasting structure is accessible to the lower levels by wheelchairs, with access along a special wheel-chair friendly route.

The **Dragonfly Pool** is a lovely place to pause on your walk to listen to the birdsong and watch the dragonflies dart across the still water. You may even see some emerge from their larval cases after the insects have climbed plants out of the water.

Findhorn Estuary

Settlements here were often engulfed by sand and eventually trees were planted to stabilise the dunes. It took a long time and the trees were often overwhelmed by sand. Digging down around stumps at **Lady Culbin's Buried Trees,** has shown that sand collected around the trees as they grew.

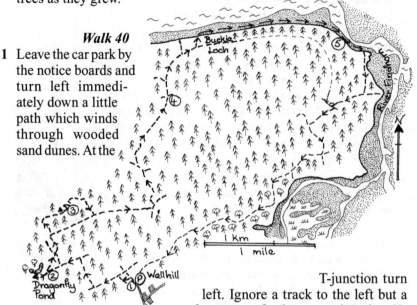

Walk 40

1 Leave the car park by the notice boards and turn left immediately down a little path which winds through wooded sand dunes. At the T-junction turn left. Ignore a track to the left but a few metres further on, at junction 42, turn right. (Many of the junctions in Culbin Forest have wooden posts with numbers carved into them; this assists greatly with direction finding) At the next T-junction turn left onto another track and go on past post 39. Where the track bears right go ahead on a path to the Dragonfly Pool, surrounded by a bank, amid birch trees. There is a seat here and in still sunny weather many dragonflies and damselflies can be seen patrolling over the water.

2 Return along the path to cross the track you came on and continue through level woodland to the next junction, where you turn left. Track junction 40 is only a short way away, and here you take the right branch, winding up the side of an old dune with younger forest to your right, then gently down the far side. At post 45 the track swings right, and just after the bend take a path on the left. Follow this as it winds up and down through the forest and then goes right and climbs steadily to the top of Culbin's highest dune, Hill 99 (99ft high) to see its splendid tower from where there are magnificent views out over the forest and along the coast. Carved into the sides of the tower is a view indicator.

139

3 Return to the path and carry on, following the zigzags down the far side of the hill, then wind right. Turn left along a track at junction 44, then left at 10 and immediately left again at 11. Keep left at 9 but bear right at 12 a few metres further on. The track now winds through beautiful high open forest. Lichens cover the ground, sometimes forming deep carpets; mossier areas are worth looking at because they may have the characteristic pinewood plants such as creeping lady's tresses or the wintergreens. Common and serrated wintergreens occur here and if you are extremely fortunate you may come across the one-flowered wintergreen. There is a memorial stone to a botanist.

4 At junction 8 go straight ahead. Ignore a track running left, wind right with alder and willow scrub to your left. Walk on past a grassy track running left but take the next one, signed to Buckie Loch, which leads into an open grassy area, once a sea inlet which became filled in. There is a sculpture of an upturned tree with a bench round it. Go down onto the beach through the low dunes

One-flowered Wintergreen

and enjoy the wild open shore, where you may see gannets and sandwich terns in summer and sea duck like scoters and long-tailed duck in winter. Walk right (east) along the beach towards Burghead which appears to float above the sea in the distance. Notice how the sea is once

Velvet and Common Scooters

more eroding the dunes to your right, undermining the trees in places. As you reach the corner, the Findhorn Estuary comes into view, and then Findhorn village. Look for seals lying out on the spit across the estuary, and in spring and summer for ospreys fishing.

5 Continue along the shore below a sandbank until the estuary widens into a pool. There are brightly painted boatsheds opposite in Findhorn village. Look for a path leading up the bank to a viewpoint with seats, then follow the track running into the forest, which keeps parallel with the shore for a while. Turn right at a T-junction, left at a Y-junction then left at Junction 3, and soon right again to junction 4, following signs for Lady Culbin's Buried Trees. The forest here is mature and beautiful. Either track from junction 4 will bring you back to the car park. If you go right you can see the buried trees, but the left track runs through more open ground on the edge of the wood, and through birch woodland in places. Here the trees are hung with honeysuckle, and speckled wood butterflies flutter along the track. Eventually the track comes back into high pine trees, to a gate. Go round it and you are back in the car park. Look out for crossbills anywhere in the forest.

Speckled Wood

Practicals

Type of walk: A long undulating ramble on good tracks and well-made paths. It is dry and sandy underfoot and it does not involve strenuous climbing. The beach is quite exposed and if the tide is very high or it is very windy this part of the walk could be avoided by keeping on along the track at the sign to Buckie Loch. Just follow the track to junction 3 where you rejoin this walk.

Complete distance:	9 miles/14.5km
Time:	4–5 hours
Maps:	OS Explorer 423/Landranger 27

Walking Scotland Series
from Clan Books

MARY WELSH has already compiled walkers' guides to each of the areas listed: material for guides covering the remaining parts of Scotland is being gathered for publication in future volumes.

Titles published so far:

1. WALKING THE ISLE OF ARRAN
2. WALKING THE ISLE OF SKYE
3. WALKING WESTER ROSS
4. WALKING PERTHSHIRE
5. WALKING THE WESTERN ISLES
6. WALKING ORKNEY
7. WALKING SHETLAND
8. WALKING THE ISLES OF ISLAY, JURA AND COLONSAY
9. WALKING GLENFINNAN: THE ROAD TO THE ISLES
10. WALKING THE ISLES OF MULL, IONA, COLL AND TIREE
11. WALKING DUMFRIES AND GALLOWAY
12. WALKING ARGYLL AND BUTE
13. WALKING DEESIDE, DONSIDE AND ANGUS
14. WALKING THE TROSSACHS, LOCH LOMONDSIDE AND THE CAMPSIE FELLS
15. WALKING GLENCOE, LOCHABER AND THE GREAT GLEN
16. WALKING STRATHSPEY, MORAY, BANFF AND BUCHAN

Books in this series can be ordered through booksellers anywhere.
In the event of difficulty write to
Clan Books, The Cross, DOUNE, FK16 6BE, Scotland.

For more details, visit the Clan Books website at
www.walkingscotlandseries.co.uk